# PATSY

# PATSY

*The Adventures of an Old Gaffer*

JOHN JEFFERSON

FERNHURST BOOKS

Over the years, articles written by my son, David, about *Patsy*, have appeared in various yachting magazines. Extracts from several of these appear in the book, and I am grateful to the editors of *Yachting World*, *Yachting Monthly*, *Motor Boat & Yachting*, *Practical Boat Owner*, the *Yachtsman* and *Small Boat* for their permission to reproduce these. The extracts from Roger Pilkington's *A Small Boat Through Holland* appear by kind permission of Macmillan; extracts from *With Capricorn to Paris* by Edward Seago appear by kind permission of Collins. I would like to thank George Millar for the extracts from *Isabel and the Sea*.

I should also like to take this opportunity of thanking David, who helped me compile the book, and my grandson, Matthew, who provided the excellent maps. Thanks too to Mike Peyton for allowing me to include two of his humorous nautical cartoons.

First published in Great Britain in 1990 by Fernhurst Books,
31 Church Road, Hove, East Sussex.

**British Library Cataloguing in Publication Data**

Jefferson, John
Patsy : the adventures of an old gaffer.
1. Sailing - Biographies
I. Title
797.124092

ISBN 0-906754-57-7

Edited and designed by Joyce Chester
Typeset by Unit Eleven Typeset
Printed by Hartnolls Ltd, Bodmin

*To the Memory of my dear wife, Doris,*
*who took part in many of Patsy's adventures*
*up to the time of her death in 1970*

# CONTENTS

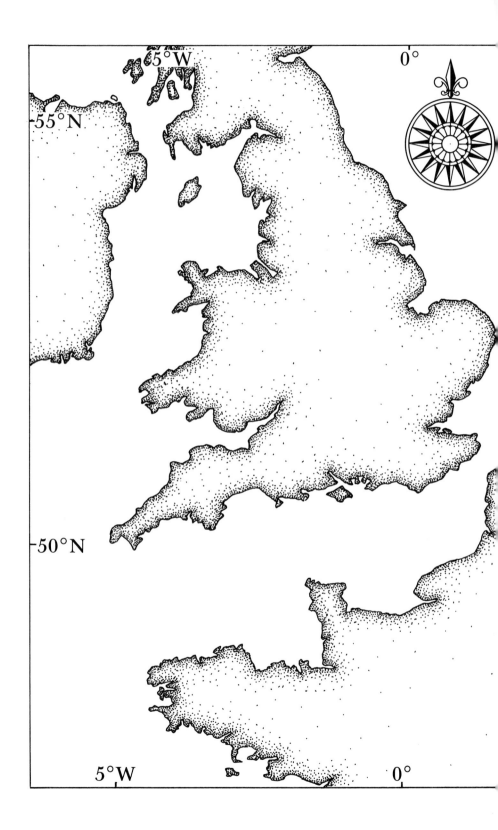

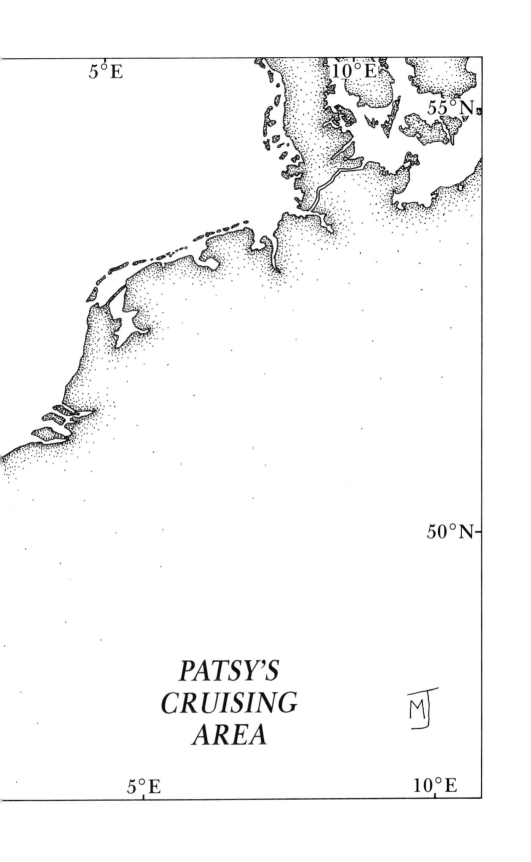

# FOREWORD

Having had the great good fortune to cruise with John Jefferson for many summers in his gaff-rigged cutter *Patsy*, Ken Summerfield and I have often sat in her snug cabin enjoying his tales of adventures and misadventures (to which we have added quite a few). We and other friends have often said 'You ought to write a book', for it seemed a pity that others should not be able to hear the story of an old Polperro fishing boat and the family who have spent most of their summer holidays sailing in her for thirty years.

To our delight he has not only written the book but has illustrated it with his own drawings. He did not set out to write a guide to navigation or seamanship, but simply to tell the light-hearted story of places visited, people encountered and adventures enjoyable or otherwise, hoping that it will be read with pleasure by those who share his love of boats and voyaging.

Oxford
March, 1990

Bill Davison

# CHAPTER 1

# HOW IT ALL STARTED

*P*ATSY is an Old Gaffer. We think that she was built in about 1912 at Looe. She is 25 feet in length from stem to stern with a long bowsprit, an eight-foot beam and a four-foot draft. There are two bunks in the main cabin and a third in the forepeak, where there is also a very uncomfortable pipecot. When we bought her in 1954 she was fitted with an old 8hp Stuart Turner engine; we now have a BUKH diesel. We use calor gas for heating and lighting. The working sails are mainsail, staysail and jib and in addition we can set a topsail and a flying jib. We also carry a genoa and a storm jib. She is moored in Birdham Pool in Chichester Harbour.

In 1950 my wife and I had had some experience of sailing dinghies and we had also chartered yachts on the Norfolk Broads both before and after the war; but neither of us had had any experience of cruising.

At that time *Patsy* was owned by Mr. Deri Evans and she was moored in Itchenor Reach in Chichester Harbour. My first meeting with Mr. Evans was at a cocktail party, where I told him how much I admired the appearance of *Patsy* and how greatly I envied him being able to go cruising. Possibly under

*PATSY* AT THE LOCK – BIRDHAM POOL

the influence of a drink or two, Mr. Evans explained that he and his wife only came down to Itchenor at the weekends and that during the week *Patsy* was not in use. He went on to say that if my wife and I would like to borrow her for a short cruise mid-week he would be happy to lend her to us. Little did he know how inexperienced we were!

We took Deri Evans at his word and on a fine day during the summer of 1951 we set off from Itchenor and sailed to Cowes. We dropped anchor in the lee of the Royal Yacht Squadron! I feel sure that this was illegal but no-one appeared to raise any objection, so we rowed ashore in the dinghy and had lunch in Cowes. When we returned the tide was running strongly in a westerly direction and there was a moderate breeze blowing from the west. *Patsy* was lying to the tide and for this reason it was very difficult to hoist the mainsail. I therefore decided to motor with a view to bringing the boat head to wind, but the engine would not start. Then I discovered that one of the jib sheets had wound itself round the propeller shaft! I went overboard in a bathing costume and tried to free the sheet, but without any success. I know now that the trick is to try to turn the propeller shaft by hand first in forward gear and then in reverse, but on that afternoon my efforts were completely unsuccessful. To make matters worse the tide was rising rapidly and to my horror I noticed that we had started to drag our anchor and were being swept gently past the Royal Yacht Squadron and out into the Solent! Again my efforts to get up the mainsail proved unsuccessful, so on we drifted towards West Cowes until we arrived off East Gurnard Buoy, opposite the line of beach bathing huts.

Here the anchor seemed to be holding, so I had a second go to try to release the rope round the propeller shaft; but again I was unsuccessful and to make matters worse I found it extremely difficult to get back on board, being in a very exhausted condition (at that time we had no stepladder). Meanwhile the wind had freshened from the west and was then blowing all of force 6, gusting to force 7. We had a drink and some supper, but with wind-against-tide West Cowes is not the best place at which to lie at anchor. Poor *Patsy* pitched and rolled and we found it quite impossible to stay in our bunks, and, as there were no bunk boards, we were periodically thrown on to the cabin sole. We therefore removed one of the mattresses and lay on the floor of the cabin, cold, damp and seasick while the wind howled outside. We were frightened that the anchor might not hold or that the chain might snap, in which case I shudder to think what might have happened, but fortunately all held. We had no distress flares, but I remembered having read somewhere that a pair of trousers hoisted to the masthead was a recognised distress signal, and therefore, about dawn, I hoisted a pair of my wife's slacks on one of the signal halyards and crawled back again into the cabin.

The slacks must have been observed on shore for, at about half-past five, a fisherman turned up in a launch with a small boy and asked what was the trouble. I explained our difficulties, and the fisherman put the small boy aboard *Patsy* and he and my wife and I tried our best to heave in the anchor, but it was quite beyond our strength. The fisherman therefore suggested that that we should buoy the anchor chain and let it go, so that it could be recovered later. Unfortunately we found that the shackle which secured the

MAYDAY!

chain in the chain locker was completely rusted up and it proved quite impossible to free it, so the fisherman suggested that we should cut the chain. There was no hacksaw on board and the fisherman therefore passed to me a very blunt cold chisel and a large hammer. I cannot find words properly to express the difficulties I encountered on trying to cut a heavy chain with a blunt cold chisel on a heaving deck. I persevered and eventually the chain parted, but it parted so suddenly that it broke the piece of string which I had used to secure a lifebelt to the chain itself, and so all the chain disappeared to the bottom of the Solent and, as far as I know, it still lies there!

The fisherman took us back to Cowes where, in calmer conditions, I was able to detach the offending jib sheet. With a fair breeze we then sailed gently back again to Chichester Harbour. Mr. Evans did not appear to be unduly upset when he heard my tale of woe and he later informed me that the insurance company had paid up for the cost of the anchor and the chain.

The morals of this story are many: firstly we should not have anchored just off the Royal Yacht Squadron; secondly we should have put out sufficient chain to allow for the rise of the tide; thirdly we should have stowed the jib sheets in such a way that they could not fall overboard and foul the propeller; fourthly of course everyone should carry flares even when sailing in the Solent. Fifthly it is important that the anchor chain is secured in the chain locker by a piece of nylon cord and not by a shackle; and finally there should always be a hacksaw on board!

Notwithstanding the disastrous start, Mr. Evans was kind enough to allow us to use *Patsy* for cruises during the next year or so, and later on, when he and his wife left West Wittering to take up residence elsewhere, he offered *Patsy* for sale and we became the proud owners.

Deri Evans was asking £500 for her. In those days that was a lot of money and all the books I had read about buying boats were unanimous in their advice: 'Never, under any circumstances, buy an old boat without first having her surveyed'. But a proper survey was expensive and I had a feeling that the surveyor would almost certainly advise me not to buy her, so I consulted Fred West.

At that time Fred was the Sailing Secretary of the Dell Quay Sailing Club and was also Secretary of the Chichester Harbour Federation of Sailing Clubs. I do not think that a nicer or kinder man ever walked this earth or sailed upon its waters. He owned a twelve-square-metre Sharpie and invariably wore a reefer jacket when taking part in races. He was a friend to everyone.

Although I did not know him very well, when I spoke to him about *Patsy*, he took the trouble to go down to Itchenor where she was lying in the boatyard. He prodded the hull and the spars with his penknife; he took up the floorboards; he turned over the engine and carefully examined the fittings. 'Well,' he said, 'You won't be going far afield, will you? With careful maintenance she should be good for another five years or more. I don't think she's dear at the price.' And that settled it!

This was over forty years ago, and she is still much used by the family. She has been sailed to Ireland, Biscay and the Baltic. In 1976 Octopus Books Ltd. published a beautifully-produced book called *The Love of Sailing*. In it are included pictures of Francis Chichester's *Gipsy Moth*, Alec Rose's *Lively Lady*, Chay Blyth and Robin Knox-Johnson's gallant craft, and a score of other famous sailing ships. On page 51 there appears a whole-plate picture of *Patsy*! How Fred West would have laughed to have seen the old lady included in such a distinguished company.

'They're more snobbish than the Royal Yacht Squadron.'

# CHAPTER 2

# ACROSS THE CHANNEL

I SUPPOSE it is true that the owners of small cruisers which are berthed on the south coast of England sooner or later get the urge to go foreign, and this usually involves crossing the Channel and making for Cherbourg. Although I have done this dozens of times I still get a thrill when I see the coast of France come up over the horizon and eventually sail into Cherbourg harbour with its back-cloth of tall, rather scruffy-looking buildings, and I smell the French smells and hear the French sounds.

Before they constructed the new marina there, one sailed into the *Avant-Port de Commerce*, dropped anchor and then led a stern line to one of the mooring buoys. The dinghy had to be launched to go ashore where there was a yacht club, patronised it seemed exclusively by the English, and there was Henri Ryst for duty-free stores.

The first time I crossed over in *Patsy* was in 1956 with Doris, my wife, my brother Arthur and my eldest son Peter. We had a very rough crossing indeed, arriving in the *Grande Rade* about breakfast time and anchored there to tidy up and have a meal. In the cabin everything was in a state of chaos, but it was a beautiful day and we sorted things out, put the blankets etc. on the cabin top to dry and then made our way into the *Avant-Port*.

During the crossing I had not actually been seasick but had taken a lot of Avomine, and when I stepped on to the quayside I felt the ground going up and down as it usually does after a rough passage. But on this occasion, to my horror, I was seeing everything in double and was not able to focus properly on either the ships in the harbour or the advertisement hoardings on the far side of the basin. Doris said, 'It's probably the effect of too much Avomine; you'll feel better when you have had something to eat.' So we made our way to the *Restaurant du Théâtre*, which is still in existence, although the square on to which it faces is now greatly changed. I found that, owing to my double vision, I was quite unable to read the menu, and the other three said they could not translate it! I cannot remember now what the other three ordered, but I chose *Moules Marinière* as I usually do for my first meal in France, not only because I like them but because they give me a feeling of having arrived.

After a pleasant meal, with a bottle or two of wine, I felt much better although there was still something wrong with my eyesight. Doris suggested that I should return to *Patsy* for a siesta which I did and slept like an angel, but to my horror, when I looked out of the porthole, I was still seeing everything double! I thought, 'Well, I must go and see a French doctor,' so I tidied up a bit and it was then I discovered that I was wearing my brother's spectacles!

From Chichester Harbour one can either go straight across to Cherbourg, setting a course between Bembridge and the Nab tower, or go westwards round the Isle of Wight, possibly calling at Yarmouth on the way. If the weather is fine it is not a bad idea to start off in the evening and sail through the night. Then, if the visibility is good, the loom of St. Catherine's can be seen astern for about 25 miles, and when one has progressed further, the loom of Barfleur comes up over the horizon.

With aids like a Seafix Direction Finder or Decca, navigation presents no problems at all. In the days of which I am writing we had no such equipment. Either because we had made insufficient allowance for the west-going tide or because prevailing winds were nearly always in the west and we had not allowed sufficient for leeway, we usually finished up to the east of Cherbourg near to Cap Levy. From there it was often a stiff beat westwards against a foul tide. Indeed I remember once having to anchor in the middle of the night and in pouring rain because there was such a strong tide ebbing through the eastern entrance that we failed completely to get into the harbour even with the engine.

Only once have we struck a full gale in mid-Channel. In 1969 we had set out from Yarmouth to sail to Alderney and when we got round the Needles we found that we could lay Alderney against a moderate westerly wind. The forecast had been reasonably good, but as darkness fell the wind increased and veered further and further round, so that it soon became clear that we could not possibly lay Alderney and would have to make for Cherbourg. As the wind increased we reefed right down, sailing with a pocket handkerchief of a mainsail and the storm jib, but after a while even this was too much and so we took in all the sails and lay under bare poles. One of the three of us was very seasick indeed. In fact I have never seen anyone, before or since, so hopelessly incapacitated. I myself was not feeling very good, but the third member of the crew was fine and he sat on the floor of the well in his oilskins while the gale howled in the rigging and the seas lashed over *Patsy*'s deck, but surprisingly, very little came in-board.

As so often happens when the weather is rough, a pigeon settled on board for shelter. It hopped about for a while in the well and then decided it was more comfortable in the cabin where it nestled peacefully on the chart table.

Meanwhile the mate, from his sickbed, stretched out his hand in his agony and encountered something warm and feathery which wriggled under his

touch. He let out a yell, sat bolt upright on his bunk, and bashed his head on the coach roof! We thought it was funny but he was not amused.

Before dawn we could see a very bright light on the French coast, but it was a steady light and therefore could not be Barfleur. It certainly wasn't Cherbourg and it appeared to me to be about where I thought Omonville might lie. When daylight dawned this turned out to be a new nuclear power station which the French had built on the hills above Omonville which I did not know about and which, of course, was not shown on any of the charts nor referred to in any of the books we had at our disposal. With the dawn the wind abated and we were able to make sail again and entered Cherbourg without any difficulty, where the mate rapidly recovered his appetite and was able to eat a splendid lunch!

On one of our visits to Cherbourg we found, to our astonishment, that we had arrived in the middle of a *Concours Musical*. There were brass bands, string orchestras, choirs, a ballet on a stage erected on the football ground and chamber music concerts of all kinds. Doris expressed interest in going to see the ballet, but that was taking place on the Friday and we intended to leave on the Thursday to try to get to St. Peter Port.

On the Wednesday evening we made our way into the town and listened to some of the music which was going on out of doors, but found the general effect rather dreary. So we wandered into the casino. Very few people were there. We went into the ballroom where there was a good dance band, but we were almost the only people present and that too was rather depressing. We were thinking of leaving when the door opened and about a dozen young people came in and nodded to the leader of the orchestra, whereupon the proceedings livened up considerably. The orchestra started to play Latin-American music and the young people took the floor. Never have I seen Latin-American dances performed more beautifully. One watches 'Come Dancing' on television, but this is always rather serious and to some extent artificial. Here the dancing was much more spontaneous and light-hearted and our evening finished a tremendous success.

Next morning we made ready to set off for St. Peter Port. In an adjoining berth lay a French motor-sailer whose skipper told us that he normally kept his boat in the harbour at St. Peter Port. He said that with the wind blowing about force 4 from the south-west we should find it very rough in the Little Russell. He had therefore decided to leave his departure to the following day, and as we were in no very great hurry we thought it wise to follow his advice. 'Splendid,' said Doris, 'we shall be able to see the ballet after all.' And this we did, taking our seats in a grandstand on the football ground. When the music started, to our joy and astonishment, on to the stage came our friends of the night before, and we were thrilled with the performance they gave!

In the days before the Common Market one had to be punctilious about the French customs. The yellow flag had to be hoisted and one presented the ship's papers at the Douane to be issued with a green card which was duly stamped by the immigration authorities. In my experience they never asked for passports. But today nobody seems to bother very much. It is true that in 1974 I got into trouble at Concarneau. We had had our green card stamped at

Cherbourg as usual, but had then proceeded to Brittany via the Channel Islands and had not re-registered on entering France again. The customs officers there demanded a fine of 1000 francs which I steadfastly refused to pay, pointing out that their attitude was not in accordance with the *Entente Cordiale*, and after a few hours' delay I was informed that they were not pressing the claim any further. But it taught me a lesson!

In the nineteen-sixties one bought bonded stores from Henri Ryst at Cherbourg. It was something of an occasion as these were solemnly put on board under the supervision of a customs officer and a gendarme armed with a revolver. Today, there is less formality. The Ryst family have assigned their business to Cherbourg Ships Stores who are in partnership with a Southampton firm, and all one needs is a yacht passport to take advantage of the twice-daily delivery service of bonded stores to yachts in the Chantereyne Marina. A customs document that has now been abandoned, along with the concession, enabled yachtsmen visiting France to buy duty-free fuel. The savings were not greatly significant, but it was worth going through the customs just to procure the beautifully inscribed and decorated document headed *République Française ... Au nom du Président de la République* and be referred to on the document as *Capitaine du Navire Patsy*. We obtained at Tréguier one of these forms which was much yellowed with age and from the concern shown by the Douanier only very rarely issued. On examination we discovered that it was printed in 1932 and referred to an Act of some six years earlier!

It nearly always seems to take much less time to sail back to England from Cherbourg than to sail there, because coming back one usually has a fair wind. We generally make our landfall quite easily though I remember once finding an adverse tide running so strongly in the Hurst Narrows that for some time we were making sternway even on the engine and under full sail.

My brother-in-law John used to say that, once, on the return passage from Le Havre, his brother Noel and I had taken so much Avomine in an attempt to ward off seasickness that we both fell asleep while on watch – myself on the helm and Noel over the chart table, and that instead of making for the entrance to Chichester Harbour he found us sailing towards Selsey! But this may be one of John's stories!

I think that a novice's errors in making a proper landfall are almost invariably due to neglect in plotting the ship's position at intervals of not more than one hour. One starts off with good intentions and for the first twelve hours or so the dead reckoning is properly recorded on the chart; but on approaching one's destination this, somehow or other, comes to be overlooked.

I remember once we were making for Fécamp. Now along this part of the coast there are no very conspicuous landmarks – no lighthouses, towers, headlands or beacons. There is a splendid drawing in the *Pilot's Guide to the English Channel* of what Fécamp is supposed to look like from the sea – the shape of the cliffs, the church, the buildings etc., and as we approached the coast, there, ahead of us, was the very thing. True, there also appeared to be a very large block of flats in the centre of the town – not shown on the *Pilot's* drawing – but I naturally assumed that it had been built after the picture had been drawn.

We stood on towards the harbour. It was very difficult to make out the precise position of the entrance; we could not see the port and starboard light towers nor could we see the masts of the yachts moored behind the harbour wall, but we continued to approach the land until we were almost into the waves breaking on the shore! It was only then that it dawned upon me that this was not Fécamp at all but Étretat! So we gybed round very smartly and shot out to sea. I am sure that had we plotted our dead reckoning a near disaster would have been averted.

Years later, in 1978, I had a somewhat similar experience when sailing through the night from Jersey bound for the Morlaix estuary on the north coast of Brittany. With me were Ken Summerfield and Bill Davison. They have sailed in *Patsy* almost every year since 1974. Both are senior citizens and both are old friends from Oxford. Bill is a very experienced sailor, a past Commodore of the Medley Sailing Club, Oxford. He looks after *Patsy*'s sailing and he deals with the engine. Ken is in charge of the navigation and he does most of the cooking. He also buys the food and acts as our treasurer.

I remember that as we approached the French coast the visibility got worse; but we were able to pick up our position by back-bearings on Roches Douvres from the Seafix.

When daylight dawned the visibility had worsened. We could still get a back-bearing of sorts on Roches Douvres but we could not raise a squeak from anywhere else. We could just make out the French coast – much too near for comfort – and worse still, we thought we could hear waves breaking on rocks, but simply nothing was to be seen. Eventually there appeared through the mist one of those brick towers, which are common in Brittany, but its colour and its name were impossible to determine. We dared not approach

'*Est-ce que tu peux imaginer un pareil accueil pour un yacht étranger qui arrive de l'autre côté de la Manche?*'

more closely as it was probably built on rocks which were uncovered at low water! So we proceeded cautiously westwards and eventually made out a red buoy. With the echo sounder turned on we slowly sailed towards it until we could read its name and by reference to the chart we were able to pinpoint our position.

Months later, a friend from Itchenor told me that on that particular day he too had failed to get any signal from Île de Batz; but we never found out why. The Batz beacon has now been replaced by a more powerful radio beacon situated thirty miles along the coast to the west on Île Vierge.

The reader will appreciate that most of the happenings described in this chapter took place in the nineteen-sixties or early nineteen-seventies. Today, now that *Patsy* is equipped with Decca, the troubles we experienced in those early days would not have arisen. Indeed, now that I am approaching ninety years of age I sometimes wonder whether a lot of the fun of navigation has ceased to exist. Sailing a small boat across the Channel in these days is much safer than it used to be – but perhaps it is no longer such an adventure.

# CHAPTER 3

# THE SEINE

*P*ATSY has cruised in the Seine no less than five times; but only twice have we made our way upstream as far as Paris. The first time was in 1960 when my wife and I were joined by Geoffrey and Constance Hope. Geoffrey had retired from the Canadian Royal Navy with the rank of Captain, and Constance and my wife Doris had been at school together at St. Hilda's Priory at Sneaton Castle.

Armed with Edward Seago's illustrated book *With Capricorn to Paris* and the 'Carte de la Seine de Paris à la Mer', we set off from Birdham Pool at noon with a light breeze from the north-east. The visibility was not very good when we sighted the French coast at about 9 a.m. the next morning. Without the modern day benefits of an RDF set or Decca, and with no features on the shore, we were uncertain of our position. Fortunately there was a fishing boat within hailing distance whose crew pointed ahead and shouted 'Cap la Hève'.

Leaving the headland well to port, we entered the Seine estuary and we made our way into the yacht harbour at Le Havre without difficulty. Ahead was a pontoon with a notice DÉFENSE D'AMARRAGER, but, notwithstanding, we tied up there and sought out the harbour master who said we

HONFLEUR

could lie there for a while.

In the spring of 1960, I did not own a proper yachting cap, and I felt that the time had come to make good the deficiency. I had therefore purchased a splendid peaked hat which made its first appearance on arrival at Le Havre. The result was disastrous. Sightseers on shore took me for an official, asking me the time of the next ferry departure, and where was there a ladies' lavatory? So the yachting cap was consigned to a peg in the heads from which it fell into the toilet!

The town centre of Le Havre was flattened by bombing during the war and has been rebuilt to a drawing-board plan; but though the layout may look good in theory, in practice it leaves a lot to be desired. The streets are *too* wide and appear to be deserted in the evening. We even had great difficulty in finding a restaurant! The concrete cathedral church is worth a visit and there is a very fine art gallery about a mile away from the yacht harbour, but little else to commend the town to the visitor.

George Millar, who sailed there with his wife in 1946, recalls post-war Le Havre in his delightful book *Isabel and the Sea*. He writes: 'We asked several people to direct us to the centre of the town, but their answers were vague. When we had been walking for a time we met a more intelligent pedestrian, an elderly man in a high starched collar. "Centre of the town?" he said, "there is no centre. This town has been destroyed by war. If we had a centre that would imply that there was a moral force already at work in the town to foster another growth. There is no such moral force. If you want to see where the old centre of the town was, then you are standing within two hundred metres of it".' My impression in 1960 was much the same as Millar's was in 1946, and it is still the same today.

In total contrast to the commercial seaport of Le Havre is the small fishing harbour of Honfleur, some eight miles upstream on the south side of the Seine estuary. No account of cruising in these waters would be complete without a reference to one of our most favoured ports-of-call. It is best visited from Trouville or Le Havre, and one should arrange to be outside the lock in good time to catch the raising of the bridge and opening of the gates.

Once through the lock, a yacht is surrounded on all four sides by most picturesque buildings. Whichever way you look there is a subject for the artist or the photographer. When we first went there in 1960 we had the harbour almost to ourselves – apart from the fishing boats. That is not the case today; but, though it is very crowded, we have had no difficulty in finding a berth alongside one of the other yachts – most of which seem to be from England.

Edward Seago writes rapturously of his first visit there in *Capricorn*: 'I can think of many moments in my life which have given me a feeling of exaltation and delight. They have not always been important occasions; some of them, in fact, have been of seemingly small concern, but they have possessed that quality which has made them landmarks in my memory. I treasure the recollection of those moments and I am profoundly grateful for them. Such a moment was *Capricorn*'s arrival in Honfleur. My heart missed a beat with excitement. It is a wonderful feeling when one is immediately and wholeheartedly attracted to a

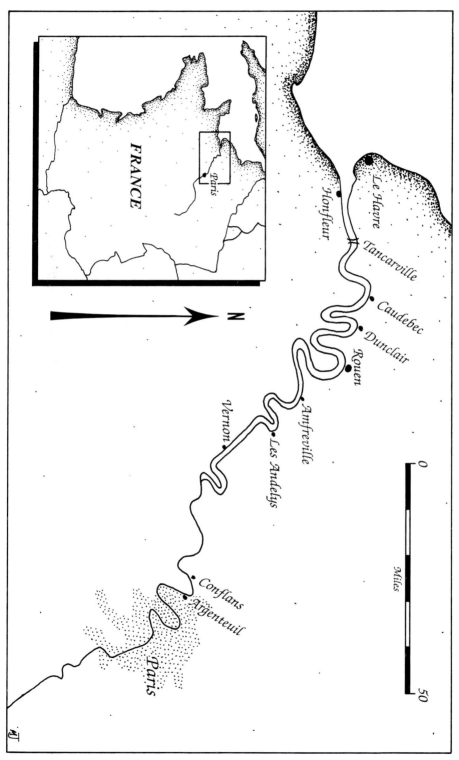

THE WOODEN CHURCH, HONFLEUR

place and the impact of that attraction strikes one all of a heap.'

Seago tells of an old sea captain he met there who lived aboard a small sailing boat called *Santa Maria* moored at the far end of the harbour. On our first visit there we paid him a call and he invited us into his cabin where we shared a bottle of wine and he told us of his adventures. Alas, neither he nor the *Santa Maria* is there today!

In the town itself there is a famous wooden church and near to it a small square in which there is an open market where we have bought excellent fruit and vegetables. There is also an art gallery noted for its collection of Boudin's paintings, and there are dozens of small restaurants. How different from Le Havre!

There is, however, a difficulty in visiting Honfleur on the way upstream to Paris. The gates open only at high water, and after motoring down the short channel and turning eastwards into the Seine, almost immediately one faces the start of the ebb flow in the river and there is nowhere very satisfactory to moor!

When we made the passage in 1960 we were not aware of this difficulty and optimistically we motored up the river beneath the Tancarville Bridge, past Caudebec-en-Caux to La Mailleraye. By this time the tide was ebbing very swiftly indeed and we could barely make any headway. Opposite the oil refinery there are some enormous circular buoys, and as there was nowhere else to moor, in desperation, we nosed up towards one of these, but could not reach its ring with our boat hook. In a flash Geoffrey climbed over the gunwale and jumped on to the buoy! Poor Constance nearly had hysterics; but Geoffrey managed to get a warp through the ring and to clamber back on board. Moored in this way we spent a peaceful night, but I feel sure it was illegal!

The authorities have now laid some white visitors' buoys on the right bank at Caudebec, but these can be uncomfortable when the tide is running strongly. We moored to one of these in 1979 and spent a very restless night indeed. I do not recommend them!

Another year, we made fast to a wooden pier which projected from the left bank. This was all right at first but the level of the river dropped so suddenly that before long our warps were almost vertical and the deck fittings in grave danger of being torn out. I cannot remember now why we could not have let out some slack and drifted sternwards but I think that for some reason this was impossible. I recall that we all donned lifejackets in anticipation of being wrecked! Fortunately our plight was noticed by some local fishermen who arrived with a very long warp made fast to something ashore and this saved us from disaster.

It is perhaps a mistake to leave Honfleur at high water and then proceed straight up the Seine until the ebb becomes too strong. It is better to slip back again across the water to Le Havre and wait there until the last of the ebb. I am now convinced that the best plan is to visit Honfleur on the way *back* from Paris rather than on the outward journey. Then one can emerge into the Seine at high water just as the ebb has started and so one has a fair tide either out to sea or back to Le Havre.

In 1960, we thought it would be fun to delay lowering the mast and to try to sail rather than to motor upstream almost as far as the first low bridge across the Seine at Rouen. The river winds all the way so that one can be running for a mile or so and then beating to windward. I rather think that in these days the authorities do not permit yachts to manoeuvre under sail and it is normal practice to lower the mast at Le Havre.

We chose to go alongside at Roys shipyard in the heart of Rouen where there are several enormous cranes; but instead of using these, six brawny dockers appeared who plucked out the mast by hand and took it away to be stored. All this cost only a very few francs and a number of bottles of beer.

Starting up river from the Seine estuary at the beginning of the flood, it is just possible for a small boat motoring at 4/5 knots to reach Rouen on one tide since there are eight hours of flood with an extended high water at Rouen. We have never attempted the passage on a single tide, choosing instead to stop off at Duclair, 35 miles upriver.

This is a pleasant place, with a friendly welcome at the *Cercle de la Voilaille de la Seine Maritime*, and a boatman to tell you where to moor. The tide runs nothing like so fiercely as it does further downstream so we have had peaceful nights here in lovely scenery rather like the Dart.

From Duclair it is only twenty miles on to Rouen which can be reached in about three hours on the flooding tide. When we first went to Rouen, the centre of the city was an unhappy mixture of bomb-damaged or decaying buildings and new development which looked out of harmony with its sur-

THE CHÂTEAU GAILLARD

roundings, but today the centre of the city is very fine indeed and well worth a visit.

Soon after leaving Rouen, one arrives at the first lock at Amfreville. Although the locks on the Seine are enormous there is seldom any room to spare. Yachts must always give the barges priority and we usually finished up tucked into the last available space at the back end of the lock.

Beyond Amfreville is Les Andelys, the site of the Château Gaillard. This is a pleasant spot, very picturesque and photogenic, in a part of the Seine where there are several islands. These must be passed on the 'proper' side – otherwise one goes aground – but the route is clearly signposted and we have never experienced difficulty.

Because of the changing depths in the river, particularly round long curving bends, barges do not always pass 'port to port' and when they intend to pass to starboard they put out a blue flag from the wheelhouse.

Les Andelys is the first stopping off place for small craft after leaving Rouen, although when we went by the little yacht harbour seemed silted up and neglected. In recent years, however, much has been done to improve the facilities for yachts between Rouen and Paris. Upriver of Les Andelys is Vernon, where the local yacht club provides visitors' moorings. When we first called at Vernon, we found the town quite pleasant, but access to it very difficult indeed! There was no quay; only a steep masonry embankment and nothing at all to tie on to. We could not anchor very close to the foot of the embankment because there were huge boulders in the bed of the river, so we had to drop anchor some distance away. From there we rowed to the shore and took with us a painter about 100 yards long, and having scrambled up the revetment, made this fast to a lamp post on the main road!

Above Vernon the Seine winds its way through the country associated with the French Impressionists; but today nothing remains of the scenes which they painted. At Argenteuil there are no small boats with white sails and even the ugly railway bridge which featured in Monet's famous picture *Le Pont du Chemin de Fer à Argenteuil* has disappeared – it was demolished in the war.

In *With Capricorn to Paris*, Edward Seago writes: 'At Argenteuil the ghosts of the Impressionists faded completely and I gazed with disappointment at the rows of factories and warehouses which lined the waterfront. This, then, was the place where they had sat on summer afternoons and painted the blue water and sailing boats with their brightly varnished masts. Where that factory rose in a concrete wall there was once a grassy bank, and Berthe Morisot had lifted the long folds of her summer dress as she walked in search of a "motif". Somewhere along that reach Manet may have moored his little boat, his floating "atelier", and Renoir painted the picnic parties in their skiffs where now a stream of tugs and barges ploughed up and down the river.'

We did however call for a drink at the Restaurant 'La Grenouillière' which lies on the left bank. We saw no signs of frogs; nor were there any ladies in white dresses carrying parasols as in the famous pictures by Monet and Renoir. All the same it was a thrill for me to stand on the very spot on which the masters must have set up their easels.

Between Argenteuil and the Paris suburbs the river banks are lined with industrial buildings including the giant car plants on the Île St. Denis; only after the first glimpse of the Eiffel Tower does the enchantment begin. A little

THE TOURING CLUB DE FRANCE MOORING, 1966,
PONT ALEXANDRE III, PARIS

beyond this famous landmark we came to the two Touring Club de France houseboats which lay between the Pont Alexandre III and the Pont de la Concorde. At that time a long length of quayside was owned by the Club and padlocked at night to discourage trespassers. The houseboats had a well-equipped office, toilets etc., a bar and restaurant and an upper deck with deck chairs and copies of *La Vie Parisienne*! *Patsy* could hardly have been more in the centre of Paris. We were a short walk from the Place de la Concorde; but although the boat was so near one was never really conscious of the noise of traffic. It was a heavenly mooring except for one thing – the wash caused by the passage of the barges and the Bateaux-Mouches made life aboard *Patsy* during the daylight hours very uncomfortable indeed. Late at night, the river traffic ceased and it was possible to grab a few hours' sleep on board.

I am under the impression that in the sixties the speed limit of the barges and the Bateaux-Mouches was increased, which made conditions on the Touring Club quay here almost impossible, and for this reason the Club have now moved their headquarters further upstream to the Pont de la Concorde, where they have constructed baffles in the river so as to lessen the effects of the wash, but even so, when I last saw these moorings they still looked distinctly uncomfortable.

The authorities have since constructed near to the Île de la Cité a new marina, which is tranquil enough but rather expensive!

However good the facilities in Paris may be today, I shall never forget the enchantment of the Pont Alexandre III mooring. We were within walking distance of the Louvre, the Jeu de Paume, Notre Dame and, of course, the theatres and the shops. We crossed over to the left bank and had splendid meals in small restaurants there and we took the metro to the Sacré-Cœur and visited the Moulin Rouge. I think it was one of *Patsy*'s most successful trips – especially for me.

When I was back on the Touring Club quay four years later in 1964, my crew left for England and I remained on board to make everything ready for handing over to Colin, my third son who was at that time at college. After a fairly peaceful night I sat on deck watching the river traffic. There were no barges because it was Sunday. It was a lovely June day – sunny and warm and ahead of me was the Pont Alexandre III with the Eiffel Tower in the background. Then along the quay came Colin carrying his kit bag and – of all things – a guitar! He was all smiles. I pointed out that with a crew of four there would hardly be room for a guitar below decks, and gloomily predicted that the thing was certain to get damaged. I think I added, rather unkindly, that he couldn't play well enough to give pleasure to anyone but himself, and I offered to cart it back to England. But he only smiled all the more and said that he felt certain they would manage somehow! I left him sitting on deck, where I had been, and made my way to the Gare St. Lazare to start my return journey.

Colin was then joined by Dick a college friend, and two girls. He tells me that each evening the four of them made their way to the Left Bank where, outside some of the restaurants, Dick played his clarinet to Colin's guitar accompaniment, and one of the girls would take round a hat while the other kept 'Cave' for the police – for the whole operation was strictly illegal! In this way they say they collected enough francs to pay for a meal each evening!

In 1960 David took over from me in Paris. He and his crew had just eight days to get *Patsy* back to Chichester. An account of this return trip entitled 'Voyage Économique' appeared in *Motor Boat & Yachting*. David wrote:

'In the Bougival lock on the outskirts of Paris, activity on the barges ahead indicated that the gates would soon be opening. All around us engines were breaking into life at the push of a button, but on *Patsy* Gerald was still swinging unsuccessfully on the starting handle.

'The barges ahead let go their lines and moved out of the lock. Feeling like a motorist out of petrol in the middle of Piccadilly Circus, I waved on the barges astern of us. They manoeuvred around us with some difficulty, a situation that did not escape the notice of the lock-keeper, bringing him out of his glass dome in a fury. Given half a chance he would have let go our lines there and then. We managed to move *Patsy* farther up the lock so that we could scramble ashore up one of the greasy ladders and then pull her through the gates, mooring her on the quay just beyond. We had not been there more than a couple of minutes when the loudspeaker on the control tower was trained in our direction. "Petit yak", it boomed, "Défence d'amarrager!" Gerald was by now well into the engine handbook, methodically working through the manufacturer's recommendations. He stripped the carburettor, played with the magneto, cleaned the filters and changed the plugs but all to no avail. The silence was shattered about every ten minutes by the loudspeaker. We were taking it in turns to swing the handle; it was oppressively hot, our hands were getting sore, and an exasperated lock-keeper was now bombarding us in English. "Little blue boat . . . *no parking!*"

'The barges going in and out of the lock had to pass pretty close to us, which is why it was an offence to moor where we were. At about 5 p.m., thoroughly dispirited and feeling we could ignore the loudspeaker no longer, I decided to beg a tow from one of the passing barges. I had hardly coiled down a rope when the gates started opening and out came a petroleum barge, the *Total Marne*. Hopefully, I waved the rope-end in her direction and to my surprise her skipper immediately put her into astern and then manoeuvred close enough for me to throw the line. It all happened so quickly that we had to fling off our mooring lines very hastily as *Total Marne* started to take up the slcak on the towrope.

'Had I not been concentrating so hard on being towed, which was a new experience to me, I would have noticed that since Bougival we had put the industrial sprawl of the Paris suburbs behind us. Bougival itself is a pleasant town with old waterside houses and a gaily coloured market stretching out along one side of the river. Beyond is green countryside, hills and trees, riverside restaurants and sailing clubs. We had been under way for less than an hour when *Total Marne* slowed down and her skipper came aft to tell us that he was shortly stopping for the night. We glided into the Port Communal at Le Pecq. This is a large barge terminal, where the crew of *Corail*, another petroleum barge, seemed to be expecting them, and they were soon secured alongside each other. We pulled ourselves up the other side of *Total Marne* and only then were we able to meet her young skipper and his wife, who acted as crew. He seemed mildly amused by our predicament, telling us not to worry, and that we could travel with him next day if we did not mind slipping at 6.30 in the morning.

'After supper, we invited our neighbours aboard for a drink. They brought with them *Corail*'s mate and his wife plus a transistor and a bottle of some fiery liquid called Mirabelle. The eight of us squeezed into *Patsy*'s cabin and with the help of the Mirabelle and our duty-free Scotch we managed to create a friendly atmosphere thick with clouds of Gauloise and the smell of garlic. The more we drank the easier it became to understand each other. *Patsy*'s cabin floor is all of 6ft by 2ft but this did not deter our guests from demonstrating their expertise at the cha cha cha whenever they could find the music on their transistor. The party eventually broke up at about two in the morning when we all went ashore to search for Gerald who had quietly slipped away earlier, in urgent need of fresh air.

'I stirred at about 7.30 in the morning and wearily poked my head out of the forehatch. *Total Marne*'s skipper appeared almost simultaneously, pulling on a shirt and pullover and looking at his watch a bit sheepishly. Five minutes later, *Total Marne* with *Corail* still alongside, was pulling us away from our night moorings. The convoy travelled at about seven knots which was a comfortable enough speed for *Patsy* and allowed us to appreciate the ever-changing river scenery, as the Seine gently weaved between lush green hills and through forests of beech trees. After Bougival, the next place of any size is Conflans which is memorable for its barges and its smell. This is where the Oise meets the Seine and for several miles the water is khaki-coloured and gives off a peculiarly pungent odour.

'We passed through four locks that day. Approaching our first one just beyond Conflans, I was a little apprehensive, wondering how we would manage on the end of a tow rope with no engine to use as a brake. However, *Total Marne* would slow down in good time, while we played with the slack in the tow rope to reduce speed. We still seemed to charge in at an alarming rate, but Gerald would leap for the nearest ladder and sprint up clutching a stern rope which he would twirl frantically round the nearest bollard to bring *Patsy* to an abrupt halt, usually not more than a couple of feet from the nearest steel topside. Only once did this procedure fail. As we tore into the lock we realised that there was no means of getting on to land and no-one up top to take a line. In desperation I hurled a stern rope towards the quayside and it somehow managed to get itself wedged in the masonry. Miraculously, it held and an embarrassing crash was averted.

'Shortly after six in the evening we entered Normandy and steamed into the last lock for the day at Garenne, fetching up for the night on a small pontoon a few miles beyond, and in the middle of nowhere. I felt a great deal happier than I had 24 hours earlier. We had covered 70 miles as against 33 on the previous day, and Rouen now seemed just round the corner. We were all more than a little weary and did not feel we could face a repetition of the previous evening's celebrations, so we decided to walk in to the nearest village for a quiet meal on our own.'

OUR MASCOT

This was the time when *Patsy* was presented with what was to be adopted as her mascot. David and his crew had returned from their meal to be met by the wife of *Corail*'s skipper who approached bearing gifts of an artichoke, prepared for eating with a generous dressing, and a little white toy horse which has hung on a hook in *Patsy*'s cabin for over twenty-five years and has, I am sure, helped bring us good luck!

We have not as yet attempted to proceed southwards beyond Paris into the Rhône and so into the Mediterranean, mainly, I think, because we could not spare the time. In bygone days the tide flowed so strongly in the lower reaches of the Rhône that the passage was very hazardous and one had to engage a pilot. Moreover the return journey with an engine of only 8hp was quite out of the question. The alternative of a tow was expensive and unattractive.

I believe the lower reaches of the river have now been canalised and the passage for a small yacht may not be quite so difficult. One year in the spring we might make this trip, leaving *Patsy* to winter at one of the ports on the Riviera, returning the following year by way of the Canal du Midi into the Bay of Biscay and so home along the coast of our beloved Brittany. It would be fun to do this before both *Patsy* and I grow too old!

CHAPTER 4

# HOLLAND

*P*ATSY has visited Holland three times. First in 1966 when we were on our way to the Baltic, secondly in 1971 when we spent over a month sailing in the Ijsselmeer and in Friesland, and again in 1983.

In the French canal system, it is almost always necessary to remove the mast in order to pass under the bridges. This operation is relatively easy for those yachts with masts housed in tabernacles; but *Patsy*'s solid wooden mast is stepped in the traditional way, so that removal can be quite a performance. Cruising on the Dutch waterways is very different, for almost all the bridges are capable of being opened, and *Patsy*'s mast can remain standing so that we are able to enjoy the many opportunities for sailing (as opposed to motoring) on the canals and *meers*.

We have never ventured across the North Sea in any of our trips to Holland from Chichester, preferring to vist the French and Belgian ports on the way there. In 1971 I was joined by Dick Thomsett and Fred Dickin – both old friends and both members of Dell Quay sailing club where Dick had been Commodore.

En route to Holland, we had put in at Zeebrugge. Although not a very interesting harbour, one can proceed from there some nine miles inland by canal to Bruges. Access to the canal is through an enormous lock, and we felt rather diffident about asking them to let through so small a vessel as *Patsy*; but they said that the gates would open in about half an hour. And so they did, and we passed through into a relatively small canal. The weather was fine and settled, and we reckoned we had plenty of time to see something of the famous old city where we planned to spend the night.

At first all was well; but gradually the water in the canal became blacker and smellier and when we arrived at the first of the City bridges, the stench was intolerable. We went ashore and had a quick glance at the city centre – which we thought was lovely and strangely enough free from smell; but spending the night aboard *Patsy* in the smelly water where she was moored was quite out of the question; so we motored back towards Zeebrugge until we came to a part of the canal which was fairly clean and free from smell. There we dropped anchor and had a very peaceful night.

Next day we thought we should see more of Bruges itself, so we returned to our mooring of the day before. I swear the smell was worse! I reckon that if one had dipped a pen into the water of the canal one could have written on paper! So we quickly made fast to a quay and hurried to the city centre.

We spent a very pleasant morning, taking photographs, having drinks, doing some shopping and sightseeing. When we returned to *Patsy*, we found

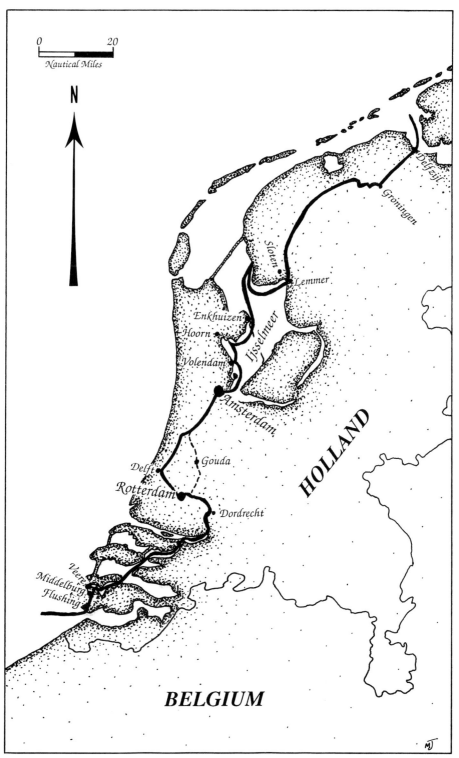

that those parts of the warps which had touched the water were covered with a thick coating of black oil or grease. It was impossible to handle them! What was to be done?

We had a modest amount of detergent on board; but not enough to cope with the offending warps. So I suggested that we should cast off and motor along the canal, towing the warps behind us in the hope that in the clearer water some of the oil might be washed off; and in this way we arrived at the Zeebrugge lock gates, which of course were closed. Before long we got the green signal and the enormous gates slowly opened. But then our engine wouldn't start! I feel sure that the reader will have guessed the trouble – one of our warps had wound itself round the propeller shaft and had tied itself into a knot. All attempts to free it by winding the starting handle first in reverse and then in forward gear failed completely!

Meanwhile the lock-keeper was getting more and more impatient; so we hastily unrolled the jib and gently wafted into the lock under sail while the lock-keeper high above us shouted to us in what I suppose may have been Flemish – at any rate it was quite incomprehensible. Inside the lock we lay against a wall and vainly tried to free the rope from the propeller shaft. By reaching down from the dinghy I could only touch the knot with my finger tips but that was not enough to do any good.

By this time the water in the lock had risen and the lock-keeper was able to talk to us face to face. He was very cross indeed. He said that a large vessel was about to enter and to occupy the position in which we were lying. We must therefore move out of the lock at once. It was, of course, impossible for us either to motor or to sail, so we threw some spare warps ashore and were pulled out through the far gates by hand. From there we drifted into a sort of backwater, where there was a thick scum of debris. My next suggestion was not greeted with any enthusiasm. This was that one of the crew (either Dick or Fred) should put on a lifejacket and sink down vertically into the slimy water until it reached chin level, in which position it might be possible to get at the propeller shaft. As an alternative, the crew suggested that if they both sat on the very end of the bowsprit it might raise the stern of the boat into such a position that I could get at the propeller shaft from the dinghy and cut the knot with a bread knife. This operation eventually proved successful!

I think it is surprising that, nowadays, in so many harbours where the facilities for yachts are excellent, accumulations of floating debris are allowed to remain undisturbed for weeks on end. I remember that in 1960 when we were moored in Paris in the lovely berth belonging to the Touring Club de France, we were at a loss to find anywhere to dispose of rubbish. There was no bin marked ORDURE. After searching about we found at the back of the Touring Club premises some dustbins into which we were about to deposit our 'gash', when some men working on the Club's houseboat shouted to us to bring our rubbish over to them. When we did so they promptly emptied the contents of our bags straight into the river!

One of the things which strikes the visitor on entering Holland is the cleanliness of everything. At Middelburg – our first port of call after leaving Flushing – we saw the good housewives scrubbing the brickwork, polishing the woodwork and treating the stone steps up to the front door with bath brick. I remember that we used to this eighty years ago when I was a child in Doncaster! I don't think anybody in England does it now. In the evening the curtains of the sitting rooms remain undrawn and, because there are no front gardens, the passer-by can look in at the family eating their meal or watching television. It is all very colourful and friendly.

We had no difficulty with passports or visas entering Holland at Flushing nor any undue delay locking into the Walcheren canal which passes through the centre of Middelburg. The town suffered badly from bombing; but it has been lovingly rebuilt with a splendid new town hall – an almost exact replica of the original.

In *A Small Boat Through Holland*, which was published in 1962, Roger Pilkington writes: 'Walcheren is one of the few remaining areas of Holland where traditional costume is regularly worn more as a matter of pride than of custom. . . . Many different styles can be seen on Market day in Middelburg when the women of the farmsteads come to do their shopping. A bodice may be stiff and starched, or it may rise high off the shoulders in fluted wings worked with embroidery. The long skirt may be striped or plain or brocaded, and there will be rows of coral beads from the East Indies, held at the neck with gold clasps which perhaps have been treasured in the family for generations. The spotless cap may be short and pointed, or there may be a spread of delicate butterfly wings of elegant lace, and often there will be corkscrew or pendant ornaments of solid gold protruding at either side of the forehead, with perhaps a blue silk bow at the back of the head.'

But when my son, David, his wife, Brigid, and I sailed in Walcheren in 1966 we saw only a few of the villagers dressed in the national costume. On the western shores of the Ijsselmeer and especially at Volendam one felt that most of the costumes were being worn as a tourist attraction. However, when we were in Friesland as late as 1973 many of the women in the remoter villages were wearing costume on market day. There it consisted of a sort of coloured breastplate made of cardboard with epaulettes to match and big white hat. The men wore black baggy trousers, clogs, and the small black pork-pie hat.

From Middelburg one sails on to Veere which did not suffer any bomb damage at all. It is a lovely town with a most beautiful carillon tower. I would have liked to have stayed on there but we were pressed for time and pushed on through the lock and into the Veerse Meer which we thought was not unlike the Norfolk Broads – or rather the Broads as they used to be fifty years ago – not at all crowded, completely unspoilt, and offering plenty of opportunities for sailing.

The Channel through the Veerse Meer is marked by conical buoys surmounted by flashing electric lanterns. Dick, Fred and I took turns on the helm, while the other two relaxed on the foredeck or in the cabin. I remember that on a beautiful sunny morning, I was below finishing my lunch when there was an enormous crash and all the plates and dishes shot on to the floor!

The channel through which we were sailing was winding and, though we

THE OLD HARBOUR, VEERE

had a fair wind for most of the way, at times it was necessary to tack. Fred, a keen dinghy sailor, at that time had had little experience of craft with long straight keels. He was negotiating one of the conical buoys when *Patsy* refused to respond to the helm as smartly as he had expected, and she collided with the buoy, poking her bowsprit firmly through the cage which enclosed the winking light. The tide then swung her gently round and broke off the bowsprit at the stem head! Needless to say the light stopped winking.

We extracted ourselves with some difficulty and continued on our journey on the mainsail and staysail only, until we came to the next village, where we sought out the local policeman and reported the accident. He spent a long time taking down the particulars, but we heard no more from anyone!

From there we proceeded through the Zandkreek, the Keeten Mastgat and the Volkerak.

In 1966, on my way to the Baltic with David and Brigid, we had difficulty in finding anywhere to moor in this length of the waterway. There was a *vluchthaven* marked on the map at Zijpe; but it had the appearance of a ghost harbour for there was not one single craft moored in the neat rows of posts! It looked so uninviting that we decided to pass on to another small harbour called Dintelsas. The wind was light so we dropped sails and motored into the twilight. Eventually we made out the red and green lights of the harbour entrance. It all looked discouragingly bleak and it soon became obvious that this was no yacht harbour but a barge terminal. We motored over to a moored barge and asked her crew if we could lie alongside. The owner shrugged his shoulders and said that he was leaving at 3 a.m. He told us that Dintelsas was no place for yachts because barges would be manoeuvring in and out all night and he advised us to proceed further up the harbour. We took his advice and moored alongside a stone quay just ahead of a tug whose skipper assured us that we should be all right spending the night there. The tide was rising and soon the quay to which we were moored was awash and I wondered whether there was a risk of *Patsy* settling on the edge of the wall! However, before this could happen the level of the water started to fall and we all turned in to sleep. At about 3 a.m. *Patsy* started to surge on her moorings and we were horrified to discover that we were facing a foaming torrent of water surging through some lock gates which were only a few yards ahead of us. Some of the strands of our new mooring warp had parted and it was only a question of time before something else might give way. The lock-keeper emerged from his office and was laconically waving his arms in our general direction. The rush of water from the sluices became worse and *Patsy* started heeling over dangerously towards the quayside. In his pyjamas David slipped the stern line, which I think saved the bowsprit from breaking. I managed to get the engine started, and then we motored flat out towards the turbulence with the result that, thank goodness, *Patsy* slowly crept forward and we were able to edge into calmer waters on the other side of the channel.

It was an alarming experience, especially at that time of the morning and our feelings towards the lock-keeper were far from charitable. He could easily have walked the few yards from his office on the quay to give us a warning of what might happen. As it was we were very lucky to escape with no more than a broken bowsprit-shroud and some badly frayed mooring ropes!

We were still in a shaken frame of mind when we arrived at Willemstad five miles further on. This is a most remarkable town, surrounded by a moat and fortifications in the form of a seven pointed star. These are described fully in *A Small Boat Through Holland* in which Dr Pilkington tells of the elaborate steps taken by the Dutch engineers to save their town from the devastating floods which have occurred there from time to time. There is a mark on the wall of a building on the quay which shows the height to which the flood waters rose as recently as 1953.

From Willemstad there is a choice of routes to Amsterdam. In 1966 we decided to pass through Rotterdam giving Dordrecht a miss. I was sorry to do this as Dordrecht is a beautiful town; but we did manage to stay there in 1973.

Half way along the Maas we arrived at a bridge which the chart showed to have a clearance of 129 + NAT (Normal Amsterdam Tide). Our calculations showed this to be enough but only just. From a distance it looked as if we could pass under with a few feet to spare but as we approached our confidence ebbed away. We asked a passing bargee whether he thought our mast would clear the bridge but he shook his head pessimistically. We put the engine into neutral and then hastily into reverse, with visions of the mast crashing down on to the deck as it struck the great steel span. Then the bridgemaster saw us. He came out of his office waving us on with an air of supreme confidence, so we moved forward very slowly. It was impossible to gauge our clearance from below – not very much, judging from the way the bridgemaster leant right out of his office window to watch us pass beneath.

Later in the year Colin and his crew approached this bridge en route to England from the Baltic. I think he must have read in the log of the anxiety we suffered in passing under the bridge. He was more seamanlike than we were, hauling one of his crew aloft in the bosun's chair where the brave fellow stayed waving Colin forward as *Patsy*'s mast passed under with a foot or more to spare!

The Noord was thick with fast-moving traffic roaring up from astern and whipping by on either side of us in an endless stream. Pleasure craft on these waters must give way to commercial traffic in all circumstances and we found it prudent to hug the bank on the starboard side and thus to keep out of the paths of the barges. On the outskirts of Rotterdam we felt rather like cyclists battling round Trafalgar Square in the middle of the rush hour! It was not much fun, so we swung *Patsy* round and cut across the river into the yacht haven at Ijsselmonde where we could brew some tea and decide at leisure which route to take next.

There are two alternatives from Rotterdam to Amsterdam – one via Gouda, the other via Delft. Having missed Dordrecht the Gouda route was the logical choice as it is shorter, virtually by-passing Rotterdam. Moreover the entrance of the Gouda canal was just across the river opposite Ijsselmonde. But we took a vote and the majority view was in favour of seeing something of both Rotterdam and Delft.

We left Ijsselmonde in good time to catch the next opening of Rotterdam's vast Koningshaven bridge. Promptly, in accordance with the timetable we had on board, the south span started to open, giving us an awe-inspiring view of the great port. We were making for the yacht basin on the north side of the river, just beyond the bridge. The contrast was remarkable. One moment we were right in amongst the dense river traffic in the busiest port in the world, and the next we were in the company of an impressive fleet of large, very expensive ocean racers moored right in the centre of the city in the quiet, secluded tree-lined Veerhaven overlooked by the headquarters of the Royal Maas Yacht Club.

Our route from Rotterdam to Amsterdam took us through Delft,

Leidschendam, Leiden and across the broad waters of the Kager Plassen. It is difficult to describe the beauty of Delft without trotting out a list of guide-book clichés. In the centre we searched for the spots from which Vermeer painted his famous pictures. The streets are lined with Gothic or Renaissance houses skirted by an unbelievable web of tree-lined canals with hundreds of small quaint bridges. We found the whole place packed with tourists, and every other shop seemed to be selling the famous blue and white pottery. But no-one can pass through Delft in a boat without stopping for a while even though it can be something of a problem finding a quiet berth.

Three miles beyond Delft, at Rijswijk, the canal divides and much of the barge traffic turns northwards towards the Hague. Amsterdam-bound traffic enters the Rijn-Schie canal to negotiate the two-mile section with its many bridges and a lock at Leidschendam which must surely be one of the oldest in Holland. It was operated with handles set in lamp-posts. A small, grey-haired man waved us into the lock. In a comic and yet touching scene, he solemnly saluted our Red Duster and then secured our lines for us, announcing that this was the least he could do for his British liberators!

Beyond the Leidschendam lock, we were able to sail for five miles along a stretch of canal free of bridges as far as Leiden. We were by this time recon-ciled to our sporadic progress, and these occasional bursts of sailing along bridge-free sections were most welcome. Anyone in a desperate hurry would find the waterways very frustrating for there will always be some delays even with the most careful planning. We soon discovered that waiting for a bridge to open is far less tedious if one knows the duration of the wait, which can be used for eating, drinking, sleeping or doing odd jobs about the boat.

At some of the bridges there is a small toll to pay, a symbolic fee of a few cents for raising the bridge. The method of collecting the toll is for the bridgemaster to swing a *klomp* or wooden clog attached to the end of a fishing line to someone standing on the foredeck; it is all done very expertly so that if you have the money handy, the whole operation is carried out without even having to slow down. Our trouble was that we were seldom prepared, and the appearance of the *klomp* had us frantically searching our pockets or the housekeeping purse for loose change. It was at the Leiden toll-bridge where Brigid, who had the purse, in a desperate bid to sort out a few cents let slip two ten guilder notes which the wind picked up and deposited in the canal. They

29

were fished out of the water by the bridge staff, and Brigid was duly despatched ashore to reclaim this soggy wealth. After that experience, we always kept a few cents within easy reach of the helmsman.

We arrived at the Kager Plassen lake in the evening, spending the night on the moorings of the Societeit de Kaag which had been recommended to us. The extensive club premises were almost deserted, but then it was the middle of the week, and no doubt at weekends the Societeit is patronised by yachtsmen in their hundreds. What wind there was next day was against us, so we tacked gently away from our night moorings, for it would have been unthinkable to motor down the Kager Plassen. The lake, with a depth of six feet of water, is about four miles long and a mile wide, and dotted with small islands. It is a natural playground for Amsterdam yachtsmen, and during the summer weekends it is packed with boats of all descriptions. At our end of the lake, there were no signs of any life apart from two small craft that had spent the night in amongst the reeds and whose crews were having an early morning swim and making breakfast.

There was more activity as we approached De Kaag, the village at the far end of the lake where we had been told we could find a sailmaker, for *Patsy*'s mainsail had suddenly started showing signs of wear and tear. The sailmaker turned out to be an Englishman who had married a Dutch girl and settled down in Holland. They both worked in a loft above the chandler's shop, living afloat on a houseboat with a delightful mooring off the smallest of the lake's islands. He examined *Patsy*'s mainsail with great care, shaking his head pessimistically. He concluded that if the head was repaired, the sail would probably get us back to England, provided we always reefed in time in a blow; but he doubted it would survive the season. He was uncertain too whether his boss would let him drop the work on hand to start our repair. We explained that we particularly wanted to pass through Amsterdam that night, and eventually he agreed to do what he could for us. With this half-promise, we whipped off the main and rushed it up to the sail loft. He then suggested that we should move *Patsy* and moor her within hailing distance so that he could give us a shout when the repair was completed. This done, we rowed over to the nearest waterside café for a drink.

We actually found two cafés, almost next door to each other, and we sampled both. The first appeared to cater exclusively for customers arriving in small motorboats and for the waterskiing fraternity, whereas the second had mostly sailing dinghies moored to the end of its jetty. We decided to stay on for lunch at the café patronised by the sailing types, and took our drinks into a large, dark and almost deserted dining room with mock beams and cages of pairs of dozing lovebirds.

On the lake it was equally quiet for there was a flat calm. Then, quite suddenly, this tranquil scene changed to one of drama and chaos. First came a few large drops of rain, then terrific lightning followed by a crack of thunder and a squall that instantly whipped up the surface of the lake into foam. From the shelter of the café, we watched spellbound as dinghies on the water were flattened by the onslaught; a few escaped, their crews dragging down their sails just in time; and one young man miraculously kept his boat up, tearing away down wind under full sail with everything flying, to the cheers of the wet spectators standing at the end of the quay.

The sudden squall was accompanied by torrential rain, and it was rather like jumping fully clothed into the water as we raced along the narrow lane until we came to a point where *Patsy* was visible. Two people were on board trying to push her off the bank with a boathook, while a third was bobbing about in the cockpit. To our amazement our ancient Stuart Turner two-stroke had already been coaxed to life and *Patsy* was starting to come clear as we scrambled aboard. 'More power' yelled our sailmaker friend who had now taken the helm. David ducked down below to fiddle with the throttle. 'Thought I remembered the old Stuart', the sailmaker shouted, flicking into neutral. He had us jumping about doing this and that, and seemed thoroughly at home standing in the cockpit of *Patsy* in the pouring rain, piloting her down the narrow channel and then coming up alongside his houseboat. We thanked him for his speedy rescue operation, and then he disappeared onto his own boat to change and have his lunch.

When we returned to the restaurant, we found the place was full of noisy, cheerful young people who had incurred the wrath of the solitary waiter by dripping water all over the floor, for most of them had finished their morning sail submerged in the lake.

It was late afternoon by the time we had shopped and collected the mainsail. The storm had passed, with the promise of a fine evening and a fair wind for Amsterdam. At one point the canal passed over a road, and it was certainly a novel experience to be sailing over the top of a busy motorway and to look down on cars tearing along beneath us. For some time we were accompanied by a fine looking German sloop which suddenly disappeared amongst the rushes down a minute channel leading into the Weinsteinder Plas. We were sorely tempted to follow, for the yachts on this large lake were moving quickly across the open water, while *Patsy*'s sails hung limp, blanketed by the trees lining the canal.

But a glance at the Waterkaart, and the number of bridges we still had to negotiate, ruled out any exploration of the Weinsteinder Plas; so we motored on, past Schipol airport, watching the aircraft circling above us with their landing lights winking in the dusk. There was still just enough light for us to make out the channel buoys on the Nieuwe Meer, another small lake with a lock at the far end which marks the outskirts of Amsterdam. Beyond was a strange shanty town on water – a conglomeration of over 2000 houseboats moored in neat lanes and no doubt providing one solution to Amsterdam's population problem. We had to wait some time outside the first of Amsterdam's bridges, but once through, the staff raced on ahead by car to open up the bridges in advance, and we felt we knew them quite well by the time we finally emerged in the city centre!

It was strange to be motoring in *Patsy* through the middle of Amsterdam in the late evening. Despite our plans made several months earlier, the nearest we got to its famous nightlife on that occasion was a glimpse of the bright lights at the bottom of roads leading off the canal. We arrived at the massive lifting railway bridge that spans the canal with a couple of hours to wait before the only scheduled opening in 24 hours which was at two a.m.! All was very

THE MONTELBAAN TOWER, AMSTERDAM

quiet, and if there was any student rioting which was then in the news, it was certainly not in this respectable residential district of Amsterdam.

Shortly before two, there was some movement aboard the waiting boats, and then, promptly on the hour, the bridge traffic lights were switched on, the red turning to green as the great span was raised. The procession of craft moved through, led by *Jesymara* – a 14-ton ketch from Ramsholt which we had first encountered in Rotterdam – then came *Patsy* and half a dozen Dutch yachts, followed in the rear by a tug towing a vast floating platform. We followed *Jesymara* which had rounded up smartly beyond the bridge, berthing alongside the western quay. Her crew kindly took our lines as we squeezed in astern of her. Engines stopped or faded away further along the canal, navigation lights were turned off, and a stillness once again settled over the neighbourhood. We bade each other good night in hushed voices and then turned in, confident we would not be disturbed at least until the dawn and the rattle of milk floats. We reckoned that there would be no more movement on the water that night, because we had been told that the railway bridge opened only once in every 24 hours. In fact this is the situation, although on *Patsy*'s return trip from the Baltic, Colin managed to arrange an unheard-of second opening! On that occasion they had missed the 2 a.m. opening after a long, wild evening ashore to celebrate their arrival in Amsterdam. The party continued on *Patsy*, which was moored in the municipal basin by the Havengebouw, and they finally slipped at about 3.30. Before the railway bridge, there is a lifting roadbridge to be negotiated, and here they roused the bridgemaster from his bed, waving an out-of-date time-table in front of him until he eventually agreed to open up. Then they came to the railway bridge and, undeterred, clambered across railway lines to the signal box from which the bridge opening is operated. What powers of persuasion were used in the signal box is not revealed, but *Patsy* slipped through in isolation at about four in the morning!

In these days, with the huge increase in pleasure craft using the waterways, the passage through the Amsterdam bridges is a very much more orderly affair. The main railway bridge, which Colin slipped through on his own, is raised for a single period around midnight each day. Craft assemble at the head of the Nieuwe Meer to leave in convoy about an hour before midnight. Inevitably it develops into something of a race between bridges with the faster boats arriving before the next bridge starts to open and then finding they have no space to manoeuvre.

Amsterdam is an exciting city to visit. There are two splendid art galleries and a most attractive shopping centre; there is also the infamous red-light district where the ladies sit in the shop windows displaying their charms. One can take a trip in a motor launch through the city's waterways which boast several hundred bridges of all shapes and sizes. The problem in a cruising yacht is to find a mooring. In the past, *Patsy* used the municipal yacht harbour by the Havengebouw or the Sixhaven harbour opposite. Unfortunately the former has now been filled in and the latter is scheduled to be abandoned for a major building development.

When we arrived at the Havengebouw harbour in 1971 we were minus our bowsprit which the reader may recall had been broken off during an argument with a navigation buoy in the Veerse Meer. Fred and Dick went off on what turned out to be a fruitless search for a boatyard which might replace the spar. Meanwhile on board I was tidying up, when a young man came past along the wharf. He spoke some English and enquired what had happened to the bowsprit. When I told him he said he thought he might be able to get us a new one, and half an hour later he returned to say that he had found something suitable! Together we walked to one of the back streets in the city and there found a yard full of scaffold poles painted white and used, I imagine, as flag staffs on carnival days. We selected one of about the right size, and triumphantly carried it back to the boat. Then we purchased a large spokeshave and a saw and spent most of the next day making and fixing a brand new spar. In all the photographs of *Patsy* taken during the summer of 1971, the bowsprit appears not varnished but painted white!

Fred and Dick finished their holiday at Amsterdam and David came out to join me. Once the crew change-over had been completed, we were underway again almost immediately, making for the Oranje lock at the far end of Amsterdam's dockland. It was the weekend, and the lock was packed with yachts and motor boats which, like *Patsy*, would be spending the weekend on the Ijsselmeer. One of the Dutch skippers, whose vast steel motor boat completely overshadowed our 6-ton cutter, went to great lengths to convince us that the Ijsselmeer must be treated with respect, for a blow could produce conditions on this shallow lake that forced even the most rugged North Sea yachtsmen to seek shelter. His last words to us were a rather gloomy warning to hug the western shores of the Ijsselmeer at all times. An elderly gentleman on the yacht next to us talked nostalgically. He was fascinated by *Patsy*'s ancient rigging, lovingly stroking a deadeye. He told me that his father hated bottlescrews and would not have them on his boat even if they had been made of gold, adding with a chuckle, 'Not that gold would have been very suitable for bottlescrews!'.

In an article published in *Motor Boat & Yachting*, David wrote: 'Verkeersbrug, the big roadbridge just beyond the Oranje locks, opens on the hour and *Patsy* was through promptly at noon. We sailed down the buoyed channel, passing the first of the Ijsselmeer's many yacht harbours at Durgerdam, and then headed towards the open water. Apparently many miles away, we could make out trees, churches and towers that seemed to be growing out of the sea, with a strange mirage-like appearance that had me puzzling over the chart and consulting the compass. A little closer, to starboard we could see the huge floating platforms which, with their cranes and piledrivers, are a permanent part of the Ijsselmeer scenery, working away to produce more great chunks of polder.

'No one can cruise in the Ijsselmeer without being aware of some aspect of the Zuider Zee works, which are slowly changing the face of this part of Holland. The actual area over which *Patsy* was sailing on that fine sunny afternoon is scheduled soon to be drained away to form the 200 square mile Markerwaard polder – the final stage in a gigantic reclamation project started way back in 1919. At that time, the prime purpose of draining off much of the old Zuider Zee was to provide much-needed additional land for agriculture, but now, more than 50 years later, the only real justification for creating yet another polder is to take some of Amsterdam's ever-growing suburban overspill. With pollution fears, the opposition to Markerwaard is considerable, and several Dutch yachtsman we spoke to felt very strongly against any further development of their Ijsselmeer.'

That was in 1971. In that year we gave Marken a miss and sailed straight on to Volendam. Here we found the main street so packed with people and coaches that it was almost impossible to move. Some of the locals seemed to have turned out in their traditional dress, mainly one felt for the benefit of the visitors. It is here that for a small fee you can have yourself photographed in

Dutch costume! The harbour itself was just as crowded with passenger boats, yachts, fishing boats and Dutch botters that are now used almost exclusively for pleasure. The working boats at Volendam still fish the Ijsselmeer for eels which are a local delicacy on sale from stalls around the harbour, and we consumed them English fish-and-chip style straight out of a paper bag.

In 1983 we did not sail straight for Volendam making instead a U-turn to port and heading for Marken which we found enchanting and completely unspoilt. The green and white half-timbered houses were very picturesque and the local residents seemed pleased to see us. But in *A Small Boat Through Holland* Dr. Pilkington writes: 'I have said that I admire Marken, but the island had two very different faces, one of which was infinitely more attractive than the other. The place was visited by a procession of trip-boats from Volendam, Monnickendam and even Amsterdam, and it knew very well that it was a show place of considerable fame. And so did the inhabitants. Never have I encountered any other place in which the people could change their character to such an extraordinary degree, twice daily.

'The Markenaars, up until nine fifty-nine in the morning, were the most natural and hospitable people. They would sit on a bollard and talk, they would show us their embroidery, they would proffer advice and help us with our shopping almost as though we belonged to themselves. The harbour master with his wooden leg, and his red pirate's sash above his white breeches, would take our harbour dues and then stay to carry on a long conversation which, as it seemed to be in some strange language of his own, was not fully comprehended by us. In fact we did not understand a single word of it, but the effect was pleasant enough and by signs and an occasional drawing on paper we managed to get along splendidly. Everybody had time to be genial and friendly – up until nine fifty-nine, at which moment the Marken Express bore down between the entrance jetties to disgorge the first hundred or more of those whose lives were being smoothly planned by Thos. Cook or the American Express.

'In a moment the place was transformed. Women who had been about their washing now emerged to stand in their doorways, putting the last curl into place before striking a noble and picturesque pose. The children who had until that instant been romping beside our bows took on their stage roles of sweet little clean little Dutch little dolly-dears. The smiles faded from the faces of the men, to be replaced by long-studied expressions of mysterious but not unapproachable majesty – certainly not unapproachable to those who had money to spend. From an easy walk their gait changed to a hand-in-pockets roll, and those who had known insufficient English to converse with us in that tongue suddenly broke into a remarkable fluency confined to certain stock phrases.'

However when we visited Marken in 1983, we saw no signs at all of Dr. Pilkington's phenomenon; the local residents were helpful and friendly and no-one was wearing fancy dress during the whole period of our stay. But we did that year put into neighbouring Volendam *en passant*, and found it more crowded than ever! We failed even to find anywhere to sit down. I remember that I consumed my smoked eels sitting on somebody's doorstep. We were glad to leave and, with a fair wind, set sail for Hoorn.

David writes: 'Although only 10 miles from Volendam, the ancient town of Hoorn is very different in character. From the sea, the place is dominated by the Hoofdtoren which is a magnificent clock tower built in 1532. There are several other historic buildings dating from the same period and many of those typical Dutch "staircase" roofs with their stepped gables and appealing facades of gargoyles, statuettes, rampant lions and various coats of arms. Many of these buildings are packed together, leaning over the narrow cobbled streets in or around the town square. The restaurant, De Waag, at the top of the very old weigh house that overlooks the square, is worth a visit. With its beams and old furniture, it has great atmosphere and is well patronised by the locals. When we dined there the place was packed; the resident pianist could only just make himself heard above the noisy clatter of enthusiastic diners.'

There was no free berth in Hoorn's marina and no room alongside the town quays so we anchored in the open waters of the Buitenhaven, off Julianapark. It is a lovely anchorage. We rowed ashore and walked through the park to the town centre where we took many photographs of the picturesque buildings, and listened to the famous street organ pictured in Roger Pilkington's book. We swam from *Patsy* in the clean water of the outer harbour and we dined on board in lovely weather. It was, I think, the most memorable mooring of all my visits to Holland.

Our 1983 stay at Hoorn had particularly happy associations. The previous

HOORN

THE FAMOUS STREET ORGAN AT HOORN

year, Ken, Bill and I had decided to try something different for our summer cruise and booked a Flotilla Holiday in the Greek Islands. This proved to be a great success. Amongst the various events organised for us by the Yacht Cruising Association was a race around the buoys for the flotilla which consisted of twelve identical Kingfishers. We reckoned we were by far the most experienced yachtsmen of the assembled company, and were confident that we would win the silver cup presented by the Association. This was not to be so, for one of the competing yachts, manned by four girls from Holland, made a much better start. Hard though we tried, we failed to overtake them. After the race we made friends with our charming adversaries. The following year, when we planned to visit the Ijsselmeer, Ken wrote to Thera Van Duin, their skipper, informing her of our intentions with the result that she and her crew joined us in Hoorn for a meal aboard *Patsy* – one coming by train, another by bus and a third on a bicycle. It was lovely weather and the party went on until late in the evening.

Although Hoorn remains a firm favourite with me, our next port-of-call was also remarkable. David writes: 'Visitors to Enkhuizen, whether they arrive in coach, car or boat, can hardly fail to be impressed by the place. A short walk along the old sea wall from the yacht harbour leads to the Peperhuis, a former warehouse used by the East India Company and now housing part of the famous Zuiderzee museum which has all the regional costumes and crafts on display. There is also a fascinating collection of replicas of the local wooden craft, together with a permanent exhibition of working and pleasure boats moored outside the museum. Enkhuizen even manages to surpass Hoorn with a great sixteenth-century double tower called the Drommedaris which, like the Hoorn tower, occupies a commanding position over the old harbour, sending the chimes of its musical carillons over the town's ancient ramparts, and across the water.'

From Enkhuizen we set sail to Friesland. There were white horses everywhere and we recalled the sobering warning we had received before entering the Ijsselmeer that one should avoid getting caught in a westerly blow off the eastern side. As we made our way towards Hindeloopen on the east shore, a particularly fierce squall hit us. We lay under bare poles while the wind howled in the rigging, but, fortunately, there was still plenty of sea room and very little water came aboard. It was all over in about an hour.

David writes: 'We liked Hindeloopen enormously. Our mooring had been allocated to us by a friendly harbour master who keeps a visitors' book especially for English yachts. It made interesting reading. The town itself is small with a square in the centre surrounded by minibrick houses, all with their bright red roofs. There is a maze of cobbled lanes so narrow that they can just take a single car, and a criss-cross of tiny waterways spanned with miniature footbridges. Sheep graze in gardens and young calves frolic on grassy dykes that almost encircle the town. In direct contrast is the new marina which has everything on a grand scale, including a vast coin-operated launderette.'

Friesland is usually entered at Lemmer, a small commercial port 25 kilometres overland to the south-east of Hindeloopen. The trans-Friesland barge traffic make for Lemmer's Prinses Margriet lock to enter the waterways that link the Ijsselmeer with the Ems estuary and Germany. The passage along these waterways towards Delfzijl, Holland's most easterly port, took us through a string of lakes and some charming waterside villages – all very picturesque. I remember being startled to see a pair of antlers moving across our

SLOTEN

bows as a stag swam from one side of the waterway to the other. When I visited Holland in 1971, I made one or two water-colour paintings of windmills. I cannot remember what became of them but in 1983 one of my nieces, when she heard I was going there, asked me to make her a picture of a windmill and of course I agreed. But when I sailed through Friesland with Ken and Bill in 1983, there were no windmills to be seen. They had disappeared! True there was one at Sloten which I photographed, but I was not very pleased with the result. What had happened to all the other windmills I cannot say.

Friesland is different from the Holland on the other side of the Ijsselmeer. The inhabitants display an independence that we might associate with the Welsh and the Scots. Those who sail these waterways fly the Friesland flag, so we bought one out of politeness and proudly hoisted it at the first opportunity. In *A Small Boat Through Holland*, Dr. Pilkington, describing *Commodore*'s passage through Friesland, wrote: 'She carried us steadily onward between rich marshy pastures and past huge low-eaved and reed-thatched farms standing stolidly in the wide fields where thin black-and-white storks prodded in the ditches for frogs, and fat black-and-white cows paused for a moment on the canal-side track to blink at *Commodore* before continuing on their casual way to the black-and-white barns where they would be milked.'

That was written in 1962. When Ken, Bill and I cruised in Friesland in 1983, we gained the same impression. I think it is the least spoiled of all the areas in Holland which I have visited. The entrance to the lovely town of Sneek is dominated by the Waterpoort – a remarkable gateway with two towers built in 1613, and I would have liked to linger there but we had not left ourselves time to do so.

We did, however, stay for a while at Sloten which is a delightful town and I have pleasant recollections of sitting in the sunshine on the edge of the canal drinking large quantities of the local beer.

We had no real adventures in Friesland; our sailing there was very relaxing, and one day I would like to return to paint; there are subjects galore!

In 1966 when we were on our way to the Baltic, we passed on through the Sneeker Meer to Delfzijl where we celebrated our arrival with an Indo-Chinese meal in one of the waterside restaurants. Brigid and David returned to England, and I was joined by my brother-in-law John and my niece Margaret. The prospect of continuing our cruise to the Baltic was exciting. Germany was clearly visible, just three miles away on the other side of the Ems estuary. Further out to sea lay the Frisian Islands which would be *Patsy*'s stepping stones en route to Denmark. We were entering *Riddle of the Sands* country.

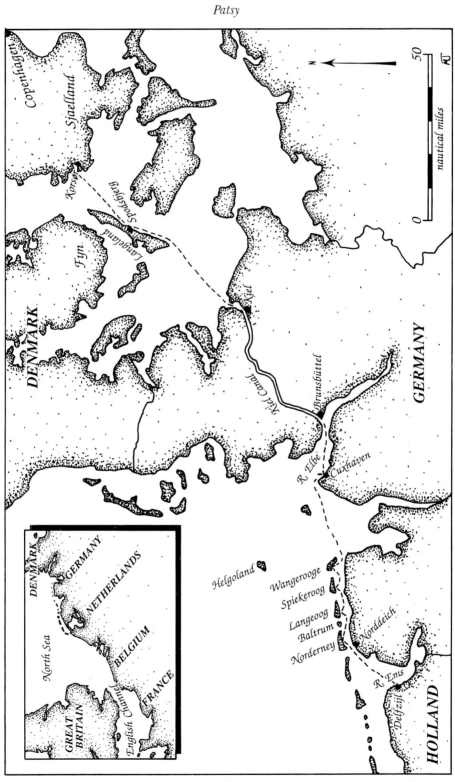

# CHAPTER 5

# TO THE BALTIC

I WAS standing on the wharf at Delfzijl, the most easterly of the Dutch sea ports. David and Brigid had departed early in the morning to return to England, and John, my brother-in-law, and Margaret, my niece were due to arrive late in the afternoon. I had spent the day on my own, tidying up and making several trips to the *wassalow* with a pile of washing.

A large Dutch motor cruiser called *Argo* was moored next to *Patsy*. Her owner and his elderly father were examining our cutter with considerable interest. The younger man spoke good English; his father did not. After running his eye over our deck from stem to stern and studying our rigging, the old gentleman shook his head and with a twinkle in his eye gave his pronouncement. His son translated: 'He says your ship should be in a museum!'

I told *Patsy*'s admirers that when my crew had arrived we intended to continue our cruise towards the Baltic, and proposed to make for the Frisian island of Norderney, 28 miles away. That was in June 1966. Looking back, I

'Your ship should be in a museum!'

cannot help feeling that the adventure was very foolhardy indeed! None of us had ever visited the area; we had no large-scale charts and there was then no 'Frisian Pilot'. I see from our log that we possessed an echo sounder, but my recollection is that we made more use of the lead line.

Our friend in *Argo* enquired about our charts and when we showed him the small-scale one which we possessed, he invited us aboard his ship and allowed us to make notes of the navigational difficulties between Delfzijl and Norderney. The passage is not easy. It would not be appropriate here to go into details; but, briefly, there is a watershed about midway in the passage which can only be crossed at high tide. Leaving Delfzijl at low water is no solution because there would be insufficient water over the sandbanks in the Ems estuary. Timing, we should have realised, is absolutely critical.

We thought we had left Delfzijl in plenty of time, as we set sail towards Norderney. The weather was lovely, with a light breeze. We hoisted the topsail and made our way northwards for an hour or more, without a care in the world. Suddenly the skipper of *Argo* overtook us. He shouted across the water that we had not allowed ourselves enough time to cross the watershed before the ebb started, and would we care for a tow?

Of course we said 'yes' and with that he came alongside, handed over the steering to his wife and I threw him a long warp. When he had made fast, his wife let in the clutch; but, alas, she let it in too quickly and the stern of the cruiser crashed into poor *Patsy* and broke our bowsprit at the stem head! In dismay, we tidied up the mess and then *Argo* towed us over the watershed at a speed of about 6 knots. Half a mile from the harbour at Norderney, he signalled to us that he was casting off. We did not see him again.

The weather had changed to rain, and partly because of this and because of the broken bowsprit, our first impressions of Norderney were not altogether favourable. We tied up at the quayside, and made our way to a shed which had been used by the German E-Boat crews during the last war. The premises now served as the island's sailing clubhouse; it was full of noisy cheerful blue-sweatered yachtsmen who made us most welcome. Unfortunately, we spoke no German at all and only one of them spoke some English. It turned out that he had been a prisoner-of-war in England. We drew pictures of our bowsprit and some of the members went out to look at the damage. They explained that we must await the arrival of another of their members who was a carpenter. When he came, he took measurements in the pouring rain and promised us a replacement spar within 24 hours. These arrangements concluded, we all returned to the clubhouse where more beer was consumed.

Next day the weather deteriorated; it was blowing hard from the south-west with the forecast of a severe gale. We consoled ourselves with the thought that even if we had had a bowsprit, we should not have been able to put to sea. We actually spent four nights at Norderney which is the largest of the German Frisian islands, being about eight miles long and a mile wide with a great lighthouse perched on the western tip. This is one of the oldest German holiday resorts, and has regular sea and air services to the mainland. It is a sophisticated mediterranean-style place, with tree-lined boulevards, smart shops and restaurants and impressively big hotels. Like the rest of the Frisian islands, Norderney's hotels and beaches all face the North Sea, with the harbour on the more sheltered but dismally bleak south side. We did make one or two sorties to civilisation on the north side, but for most of our stay we had to content ourselves with an occasional quick dash between rain squalls to the clubhouse.

It was late afternoon and less than 24 hours after our arrival at Norderney when who should arrive in the pouring rain but the carpenter, wheeling his bicycle on which rested our replacement bowsprit. It looked like a cut-down scaffold pole and we hoped that he had not stolen it; but he was kindness itself and refused to accept any payment – only beer! Imagine our disappointment when, the following morning, we set about fixing the spar in position only to discover it was three feet too short! What was to be done? The luff of our jib was too long to allow it to be set from such a short spar; and to extend the latter by scarfing on a piece of our broken bowsprit would be very difficult indeed. Moreover we had no suitable tools. Unwilling to admit defeat, we tried to borrow some from a club member who spoke a little English. He said what we were trying to do was impossible and that he would tell the carpenter of our dilemma.

To our astonishment, a few hours later, the carpenter came back again with a longer spar which turned out to be satisfactory in every way. Still no payment was required so we all retired to the yacht club where yet more beer was consumed. The members produced a Visitors' Book containing some famous names amongst the entries of foreign yachts that had put into the harbour over the past 20 years or so. I spent some time making, for our contribution to the book, a water-colour drawing of *Patsy* with her broken bowsprit. This was greatly admired by the club members, and when it was finished several more rounds of beer were called for. It occurs to me that if any reader calls in at Norderney, they would do me a favour if they enquired about the Visitors' Book to discover if the picture of *Patsy* is still in existence.

It was fine and warm the next day which was spent applying two coats of varnish to the new bowsprit and fixing it in position. The club was strangely deserted, and then we discovered the reason – they had sold out of beer during the last two days when the appalling weather had driven all the local yachtsmen under cover. Now, with a good forecast, we could continue island-hopping eastwards which we thought might be a slow process as, off each of the islands, is a watershed which can only be attempted around high water. The alternative to this inshore passage-making would have been to pass to seaward of the islands where the WNW gales would have built up a considerable swell.

We decided to sail inshore, but our start from Norderney was hardly auspicious. We left at 6.30 in the morning, and grounded twenty minutes later (fortunately only briefly) just outside the harbour entrance. We managed to cross the watershed more than an hour before high water although the echo sounder revealed that there was often less than two feet depth beneath us. We reckoned we had just sufficient time to cross the next watershed off Baltrum before the water started running out, and it was with some relief that we reached the deep water between Baltrum and Langeoog where we were able to enjoy a gentle sail.

We soon discovered a drill for making a passage from one island to another. This meant leaving about three hours before high water and nosing up the channel, leaving the withies to port and the buoys to starboard. *Patsy* touched bottom all too frequently, sometimes sticking in the soft sands. As soon as we grounded we would lay an anchor over the stern, wait until we floated off and then nudge forward until we grounded again. This procedure we found much better than running the chain over the bows because, anchored in that manner, when *Patsy* floated she would have swung round to face the flood, and we would then have had to turn her in the very narrow channel to continue. The only real problem we met was where we came to a junction marked by withies with no clear indication as to which channel we should follow.

Having arrived at Langeoog without further problems, we were able to spend about six hours in the harbour which, in the First World War, the Germans used as a seaplane base. It was there that *Patsy* was boarded for the first time by German Customs. The officer, who was courteous, but not particularly friendly, demanded to know the location of our bonded store. We shook our heads, indicating that we had none. He then enquired whether we had any spirits on board. We produced about a bottle and a half of gin and a bottle of whisky. He then insisted that the spirits must be in a sealed container. Eventually a pillow case was produced which he set about stringing up. He was on the point of applying his official lead seal, when he delved into our makeshift bonded store and retrieved the half bottle of gin, saying he would leave this out for us!

We met some interesting boat owners at Langeoog. One was a single-hander who always spent the summer months sailing his small yacht in the Baltic, and the winter months sailing in the Mediterranean and along the North African coast. In another small boat were two young men tracing the voyage of *Dulcibella* as featured in Erskine Childers's *Riddle of the Sands*. They had tried to get various companies to sponsor their enterprising trip, but only Cadburys had contributed by donating a whole case of Marvel dried milk which was far more than they needed; so they kindly passed on a couple of tins for *Patsy*'s stores. We walked the mile into town in the afternoon; the island reminded me a little of Selsey, on the south coast of England.

We were perhaps too prompt in our departure time from Langeoog for the watershed was only 4 miles away. There was not enough water in the channel and, although we followed the lines of withies with care, we spent much of the first two hours grounding and waiting for a rise of water. The lead line never showed more than a foot under the keel. Once over the watershed we made good progress to the next island called Spiekeroog, entering the harbour in the late evening, where we spent a peaceful night with *Patsy* dried out alongside the island's ferry boat.

Next morning we made an early start for Wangerooge – the most easterly of the Frisian islands. We found following the birch trees difficult in this section for there are two west–east channels and then a confusion of marks off Wangerooge's harbour; we were nevertheless safely alongside in less than three hours after leaving Spiekeroog.

I am told that in recent years there has been considerable improvement in the facilities ashore for yachts visiting the Frisians. It was a different story when we were there. At Wangerooge we had to beg fresh water from the crew of one of the ferry boats, and at Langeoog, where we ran out of petrol, a man kindly offered to take a couple of our jerry cans over to the mainland to the nearest garage. Wangerooge's town is about 2 miles from the harbour and reached by means of a small railway which John and Margaret took in the morning to have a look at the popular holiday resort on the north side. In the afternoon, we walked over to the western tip of the island for a view of the channel at low water. Looking at our chart, it certainly appeared feasible to leave Wangerooge's harbour and put straight out to sea for the 40-mile passage round into the Elbe and then up the river to Cuxhaven. This seemed shorter and preferable to attempting the inshore passage behind the island.

But viewed from a high point on the western end of Wangerooge, the passage out to sea looked most intimidating. Where we thought the channel between the two islands should have been was all breaking waves! We had worked out that to catch the flood up the Elbe we should have to leave about midnight, but a couple of hours before then, John got into conversation with a local yachtsman who strongly advised taking the inner passage, starting an hour earlier. He said that the withies were not far apart and that with a decent light we could pick our way from one birch tree to the next without any difficulty. We decided to take his advice; but imagine our frustration when we found the Aldis lamp would not work! We spent until midnight struggling with repairs to both the Aldis and the compass light with no success at all. Our Cadbury-sponsored friends from Burnham, who had arrived at tea-time, decided to do the inshore passage that night and slipped out of harbour at midnight. It was a most beautiful evening with a large yellow moon; night sailing would have been a real pleasure!

We had to put off our departure from Wangerooge until eleven the following morning, which turned out to be very still and hot with hazy sunshine. We passed over the watershed without difficulty and soon identified a long breakwater to starboard which we had been warned might present something of a hazard at night. From then on it was deep water all the way and we enjoyed a sense of relief, having been in the shallow waters between the Frisian islands and the mainland for the best part of a week.

At last we were sailing again, with a light easterly breeze that allowed us to point a course from buoy to buoy, across the estuaries of the Jade and the Weser towards the Elbe light vessel. Here we had to alter course and beat gently up the Elbe estuary with the flooding tide. Although there was still only a light breeze, the water was surprisingly rough and I could imagine that there might be very uncomfortable conditions in a strong wind against the tide. We know now, but we did not know then, that we were only a few miles from the spot where *Dulcibella* of *The Riddle of the Sands* was nearly shipwrecked, having been lured into a cul-de-sac by the villain of the story. It was nearly dark when we reached Cuxhaven. We managed to locate the yacht basin; but only with some difficulty because of a confusion of shore lights. Then we had a quick change and went ashore for a reasonable meal at a small rather scruffy harbour restaurant.

Continuing up the Elbe from Cuxhaven, it is surprising how far one goes up the river with land on one side and nothing but a vast expanse of sandbanks on the other. The entrance to the Kiel Canal – the fifty-mile waterway that links the North Sea with the Baltic – was much less formidable than I had expected. It is at Brunsbüttel. Here I went into the office to pay the very modest dues while John and Margaret shopped for some much needed provisions. Parts of the canal wind through some very lovely countryside, and it is an unusual experience to share such tranquil surroundings with 15,000-ton liners. Pilotage is not necessary for yachts below 50 tons, but without a pilot vessels can only move between sunrise and sunset and in good visibility. Sailing in the canal is permitted; but a motor may also have to be used to maintain a minimum speed of 6 k.p.h. Tacking is definitely verboten. Tows can usually be negotiated with the skipper of a coaster; but they travel at about 8 or 9 knots and I thought that the prospect of hanging on to *Patsy*'s tiller going at that speed for hour after hour was more than my nerves would stand.

Until one gets used to it, passage along the canal can be hair-raising. All traffic, of course, passes port-to-port; but the adrenalin flows rapidly when one is being overtaken by some vast liner with only a few yards to spare between her topsides and the bank of the canal. The traffic is controlled by lights mounted on big towers. They are not like simple road traffic signals but a combination of several red, green and white lights and we were totally confused as regrettably we had mislaid the guide we had been given at the lock. On one occasion the lights came on and nothing seemed to be moving in our direction, so we stopped for a while until a motorboat came by. We signalled to ask him if we could follow him but he waved a negative to us, although later we realised he probably thought we were requesting a tow!

We had decided that there was no hope of passing through the canal in one day, and there seemed to be only one place for a night stop which was just past the 40-kilometre mark, in the smaller Gieselau canal. After a peaceful night there, we were off in good time the next day, reaching the enormous lock at the far end of the canal by early afternoon. There was a queue of shipping waiting to enter, but after all the merchantmen had gone into the lock in front of us, the lights changed. We were uncertain whether or not we should proceed; but a man at the end of the lock waved to us to enter, directing us to squeeze in under the stern of a big steamer.

The level of the water in the lock changed imperceptibly and we motored out into the Baltic, the last of the convoy. With some difficulty we found the British Kiel Yacht Club where we were directed into a berth by a soldier. The Royal Engineers had a large maintenance unit here and the very splendid yacht club was at that time used primarily for the recreation of the officers and men serving in Germany. We went up to the clubhouse where we were met by the Major-in-charge. He made us very welcome and explained that the place was rather crowded because the Kiel Regatta would be taking place on the following day. We felt very scruffy in such magnificent surroundings and *Patsy* looked out-of-place amongst the sleek racers with their warps beautifully coiled down on their spotlessly scrubbed decks. Nevertheless, the Major invited us to dine that evening at the Club if we did not mind waiting until the staff had dealt with a formal dinner for the competitors.

We took the advice of some members of the Club as to which was the best of two or three alternative routes towards Copenhagen. It was strange not having to plan our departure to tie in with the local tide tables, as we headed out into Kiel Bay, making for the Langelands Belt. We realised that there would hardly be time to reach the Great Belt and then sail round the top of the island of Sjaelland, past Hamlet's Elsinore and towards Copenhagen. We had spent too long in the Frisians, but reckoned we could still get to within 40 miles or so of the capital where we could meet various Danish relations. This was to be the highlight of the cruise for John who is half-Danish and had always wanted to take *Patsy* into these waters.

The wind was light and flukey, but none of us really wanted to start the engine as we basked in the sunshine enjoying our first sail in the Baltic. Eventually the wind fell away altogether and at noon we were forced to motor, making for the little harbour of Spodsbjerg on the island of Langeland. Here John wanted to telephone his relations to tell them of our whereabouts. Although most people in Denmark speak some English, the elderly couple who ran the local post office did not; but two small children came to our rescue! John's cousin was contacted who said he would meet us at Korsør, a sail of about 20 miles from Spodsbjerg and little more than an hour's car drive from Copenhagen.

A lady who was on the quay at Spodsbjerg when we arrived and who helped us with our lines, asked us if, when we left the harbour, we could hoist our sails as she would like to photograph *Patsy*. Evidently gaff rigs and brown sails were a most unusual sight in Denmark! We tried to oblige, but she must have been disappointed for off the harbour there was insufficient wind even to fill

*THE LITTLE MERMAID*, COPENHAGEN

the sails. However, clear of Spodsbjerg, we were able to switch off the engine and hoist all the canvas including the topsail; then, a short time later, not only had we to drop the topsail, but, as the wind was picking up alarmingly, put three reef rolls in the mainsail. In no time we found ourselves in short, steep seas, but we were still making rapid progress. Then, a few miles from Korsør, the wind dropped as suddenly as it had risen, and once again we were on the engine. At least we had had a taste of the notorious fickleness of the Baltic weather!

We had arrived at Korsør earlier than anticipated, so John asked one of the members of the yacht club to phone his cousin Eric who, in less than an hour, appeared with his small boy to transport us to the comforts of proper beds, hot baths and leisurely meals around the dining room table. For me it was the end of six continuous weeks of living and cruising in *Patsy*; but before taking the ferry back to England, we were able to savour delights of Copenhagen including, of course, an inspection of *The Little Mermaid* and an evening in the enchanting gardens of the Tivoli.

## THE RETURN TRIP

Within two or three days of our arrival at Korsør, Colin had set out from England with five weeks in which to sail *Patsy* back to the south coast. His cruise turned out to be something of a struggle against the elements, in an endeavour to keep to a tight schedule.

His log reads: '. . . out of the 23 days we have been sailing since we left Korsør, only on 8 of these did the wind not exceed force 6, and out of the 8, the wind was in our teeth for 6 of them, giving us just two days of easy sailing . . .' By that time they had only reached the Ijsselmeer.

When Colin was joined by his crew, Pat and Julia, at Korsør, their immediate departure was postponed, for it was blowing force 6 from the west, but next day the wind appeared to have dropped, so they set off for Lohals on the northern tip of Langeland. Then the wind returned to Westerly 5–6, and they had a beat all the way, covering the 15 miles in 10 hours!

The next port they wanted to visit was Bagenkop, right at the other end of Langeland, where they had arranged to meet up with the fourth crew member. The wind had backed to south-west, still force 6, so they resigned themselves to a stiff beat to windward along the east side of the island. Given a fair wind they could have covered this 30-mile passage in 6–7 hours; as it was, they left Lohals at 8.20 a.m. and nineteen hours later, at about three in the morning, they had only reached the southern end of Langeland where *Patsy* was making no progress to windward at all! Colin's crew had all turned in and he felt thoroughly dispirited, particularly as the harbour lights of Bagenkop were visible only a mile or so off. Realising he was fighting a losing battle, he bore away and shot back to Spodsbjerg. So, on their second passage, they had progressed a mere 16 miles in 23 hours! According to their provisional schedule they should by then have reached Kiel. With the weather still SW 5–6 and locals talking of possible gales, they travelled to Bagenkop by bus.

The following day the wind had dropped completely and, being two days behind schedule, the urge to press on regardless became dominant; so they cleared Customs and motored up to the southern end of Langeland. Here they picked up a gentle north westerly, and were able to stop the engine and to set all the sails. To add to their pleasure, the constant rain of the first three days gave way to brilliant sunshine which stayed with them all the way up the Kiel Fjord to the British Kiel Yacht Club.

The start of their second week found them making good progress under sail along the Kiel Canal which they covered in less than 24 hours. At Brunsbüttel, the girl who had joined them at Bagenkop made some polite excuse and announced she was returning home. Pat saw her off and returned to *Patsy* with two Italian seamen who were in search of a tow. They introduced themselves as Guido and Franco who were the owners of a magnificent Bermudan sloop called *Dido*. They had bought the hull in Norway where they had rigged it and were endeavouring to get her back to Genoa. Their immediate problem was to manoeuvre out of the basin and through the Brunsbüttel lock without an engine. Colin tried in vain to assist, but there was by then a gale force wind to contend with, so the operation was postponed until the following morning.

The next port-of-call was Cuxhaven where they moored between the Italians' sloop and a boat belonging to the local member of the Cruising Association who was most hospitable, entertaining both crews to dinner at his home. They were now within range of the BBC Droitwich transmitter; but that gave them no comfort at all for they were forecasting gales for sea area Thames. They left Cuxhaven in a light north westerly, reaching the Elbe 2 lightship early in the evening where the wind dropped completely. Motoring, they caught up the Italians who gratefully accepted a tow. Then the wind increased, so they slipped *Dido*, deciding to put in long tacks through the night to reach Helgoland. This isolated island 28 miles off the German coast is a duty-free haven which attracts a regular stream of liners, disgorging bargain-hungry tourists in their thousands. *Patsy*'s crew were grateful to be on terra firma for a while, but not greatly impressed with the place which they likened to a large new town shopping-precinct.

With a forecast of North 5, Colin wanted to slip from Helgoland at 4 the next morning to catch the tide, but his crew threatened mutiny and it was noon when they finally departed, tacking into a moderate wind. They had been hoping to make Norderney, but the wind gradually increased and their progress to windward was depressingly slow. After 24 hours at sea, they were still some way off, and the prospect of another night bashing into the head wind did not appeal, so instead they made for the harbour at Langeoog, settling in a drying berth in the soft mud as darkness fell. The log records that they had covered only 35 miles in 33 hours!

At the start of their third week, *Patsy* was back in *Riddle of the Sands* territory. They decided to make for Norderney along the inshore channels, negotiating the watersheds at both Baltrum and Norderney on the same tide as we had done coming the other way. All went according to plan until they were about two miles off Norderney's harbour, when a gust hit them at the precise moment they reached the place where the channel divides. In the confusion, they followed the wrong set of withies and grounded in the Wagengat. By the time they had floated off in the afternoon, the wind was force 7 from the West. Fortunately there was still some shelter from the islands and they were able to make half a knot by motoring flat out against wind and tide, reaching Norderney at tea-time.

They allowed themselves 24 hours on the island, and who should turn up just before they left but our friend the carpenter, who presented his compliments along with an invoice for a new bowsprit! Colin thanked him for the excellent job he had done, and paid over what seemed to be a very reasonable sum.

Colin was faced with the same problems *Patsy* had encountered on the way out – the crossing of the watershed off Norddeich and then negotiating the shallows in the Ems estuary. After leaving Norderney, they spent part of the night leant over at 60°, aground off Norddeich. Floating off by 4 a.m., the wind actually allowed them to sail along the narrow channels and over the watershed at six in the morning as planned. But, by the time they had reached the point where it was necessary to cross the drying sandbanks to enter the Ems river proper, the tide and a rising force 6 wind were against them. Colin became concerned because, particularly with the deteriorating weather, this was no place in which to be caught at low water. A barge appeared, and Pat waved a tow line at the skipper which fortunately he accepted. With little time to lose, the barge charged ahead at an alarming 7 knots, causing Colin considerable anxiety at *Patsy*'s helm; but as soon as they were in the Ems, and the soundings were again reading in fathoms, they let go the tow and within an hour had reached the safety of Delfzijl.

By now they were all feeling very tired and distinctly grubby, so although they were more than a week behind schedule, they allowed themselves the luxury of 24 hours to recuperate. Offers of showers at the *Seemanshuis* were gratefully accepted after which they spent the evening there watching television! The next day when they returned from shopping, who should they find moored next to them but their Italian friends Guido and Franco. Without an engine, they had not been able to sail inside the Frisian islands, and had had a rough time trying to make the entrance to the Ems, battling for several days against force 6–7 winds. They gratefully accepted *Patsy*'s tow through the lock leading into the Ems canal and the start of the Dutch waterways.

By evening they had reached Groningen along with the Italians, who were very grateful for the odd tow when the wind dropped, but Colin sensed that they were not all that keen on this inland navigation without an engine. The following afternoon, another crew member, Jenny, was due to arrive at Schipol Airport which serves Amsterdam. So Colin decided that, in spite of the many delaying bridges to be negotiated, they should attempt to rendezvous at Grouw, some 30 miles further along the waterways.

He managed to persuade a particularly helpful girl in the Groningen tourist office to convey details of *Patsy*'s schedule for Jenny to pick up at Schipol, and then they departed with all haste, realising that they might have been somewhat optimistic in their calculations. Two railways bridges and a lock later, as they headed towards the Bergumer Meer, the Italian boat went aground and *Patsy*'s engine was overheating. Having cleared weed from the propeller and cooling water inlet, they were ready to set off again when a barge came along and both crews gratefully accepted the offer of a tow. The bargee took them through the Bergumer Meer and on to Suawoude where the routes parted. Colin handed over a half bottle of whisky by way of appreciation, and the barge headed off towards Leeuwarden. *Patsy* and *Dido* stayed for the night where they had been dropped, but by morning Colin had to say goodbye to the Italians, reluctantly leaving them to cope with a force 6 wind in their teeth. He and his crew were sad about this because they had enjoyed their company; but *Patsy* had a tight schedule; the Italians had not.

The farewells proved to be somewhat premature. *Patsy* proceeded to Grouw with all speed, and her crew just managed to get to the station in time to meet Jenny; but when they returned who should have arrived but the Italians who had quickly managed to secure a tow! Grouw, which is an attractive yachting centre, was so popular that Colin was unable to persuade his crew to leave until the following afternoon. They then had one of their very few really good sails on the waterways, along the Prinses Margriet canal and across the Sneeker Meer, in the company of *Dido*. They were entertained that evening by Guido and Franco to spaghetti and wine. Next day the wind had returned to its customary force six in their teeth, so they set off with *Dido* in tow and then soon hitched a pull from a passing barge which towed them the last lap across Friesland.

At Lemmer yacht haven, they waited in vain for a shift in the wind; but when the weather had eased sufficiently for them to motor, they again bade farewell to Guido and Franco, and crossed the Ijsselmeer to Enkhuizen. Three days later, they were moored up right in the centre of Amsterdam. In the previous chapter, reference is made to Colin having to round up his crew in the early hours of the morning, and then, with several additional passengers, motor round from the yacht basin into the canal. He then had to persuade the bridgemaster of Amsterdam's main railway bridge to open up. It was during their revelry ashore, that Julia and Jenny were made an offer they could not resist! This was the use of a comfortable flat with all mod cons in Amsterdam. The skipper was then informed that two members of his crew would be jumping ship!

Colin and Pat tried to console themselves that they would then be able to get in some serious sailing with only just over a week to be back in England. They took the Gouda route to Rotterdam, but failed to get through the railway bridge there in the evening, and as the next day was Sunday with no bridge opening, they were stuck there until 5 a.m. on the Monday morning. They then made good progress through Dordrecht with night stops at Willemstad and Veere. There were almost continuous gale warnings from then on, and an entry in the log at Veere records that they had just three days left with 94 miles still to go to Dover.

At Flushing they met up again with their Italian friends, Guido and Franco, who had found progress through Holland without an engine too difficult. They were on their way home, having left *Dido* in the Ijsselmeer. *Patsy* managed to dodge the gales and, with short stops at Blankenberge and Calais and two nights spent at sea, she made Dover on schedule. The rest of the family felt that this was no mean achievement.!

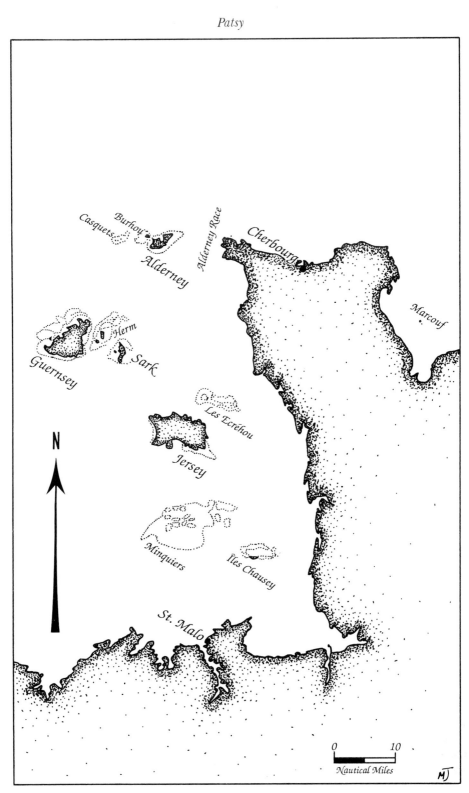

# CHAPTER 6

# ISLANDS IN THE CHANNEL

F OR all of us, islands have a particular fascination. There must be a dozen or more all within a hundred miles of our home port of Chichester. Over the past thirty years, we have visited most of them, ranging from tiny rocky outposts like the Ecréhous and the Minquiers to the large holiday resorts of Guernsey and Jersey.

## ALDERNEY, BURHOU AND CASQUETS

Our first passage to Alderney was in 1956. We had set off from Cherbourg in lovely weather; the sky was blue and there was a fair wind from the east. The distance to Braye (the only harbour on the island) is about 25 miles and we expected to be there by tea-time.

We had splendid sailing with a clear view of Cap de la Hague to port and, later, the outline of Alderney ahead. We were slowly overhauling a Bermudan sloop which looked to be about the same size as *Patsy*. Now although a Bermudan rig is normally faster than a gaff rig when going to windward, a gaff rig comes into its own when sailing off the wind, and we felt that it would be fun to try to overtake; so we set the topsail. With a clear view of Quenard lighthouse, we followed the sloop, steering a course to leave the point well to port. But when we got within about half a mile of the shore, it was obvious that both *Patsy* and the sloop ahead were being carried southwards into the Alderney Race which surges down the eastern side of the island. We both turned to the north, but by this time the strength of the tide had increased considerably and, even with the engine running flat out, we were proceeding backwards! So the idea of entering Braye was abandoned, and instead, we went about with the intention of letting the Race carry us southwards towards Jersey. To my horror, immediately ahead of us there reared up an enormous wave which looked about 12 feet high and which crashed down on the foredeck! We were almost overwhelmed, when another of similar size followed. I think a third one would have swamped us, so I immediately bore away, and once more we were being swept backwards, with the crew pumping like men possessed.

Over towards the shore, the water looked a bit calmer, and I thought it might be just possible to make a little progress in that direction. The tide slacked off and, using the engine, we were eventually able to reach Braye.

It was a salutary lesson to avoid wind-against-tide conditions in these waters which could have been achieved by steering a course much further to the north to reach Alderney. Years later, David made precisely the same mistake and wrote about it in an article for *Yachting Monthly* published in January 1988: '. . . We had taken over *Patsy* in Cherbourg. Our start was hardly auspicious with the classic navigational error on passage from Cherbourg to Alderney. Visibility was poor, so we hugged Cap de la Hague and then set a course 45° above the direct line across the Alderney Race to Braye. We should have been at least three miles off Cap de la Hague, and in no time we were being sucked into the Race, and motoring flat out due north in a hopeless attempt to stem the tide which was determined to carry us swiftly down to Jersey. The only consolation was that three other yachts, also from Cherbourg, had made the same mistake.

'The children realised that all was not well as I took bearings every few minutes, before becoming more and more dispirited. Then we spied a yacht very close to Alderney and making good progress along the coast in the opposite direction to the fast flowing Race. This back eddy is clearly marked on the *Admiralty Tidal Stream Atlas (NP264)*, but it has to be seen to be believed. Although it stops abruptly half a mile south of Quenard Point, it provided me with a great face-saver as we slewed across the Race and then took the eddy up to Longy Bay where we anchored for a bathe and tea, until we could take the first of the north-going tide round the corner into Braye Harbour. . . .'

Navigation is no easier on the north-western side of the island where there is another tidal race known as the Swinge. On one occasion we had reached the south-west tip of Alderney, heading northwards towards Braye in slack water. We actually got within a quarter of a mile of the harbour breakwater when the tide turned against us. Even with a fair wind and the engine going all out, we were making no headway at all, and, with no proper steerage way, *Patsy* nearly piled up on the rocks off Burhou before we got her round and under control. Then we drifted back down the Swinge, anchoring in calm water where we waited for the tide to turn.

There are really no excuses for missing the north-going tide in the Swinge if coming up from the other Channel Islands. It is simply a question of allowing enough time for the passage. On David's first cruise in *Patsy*, when he visited the north coast of Brittany and the Channel Islands, he had set sail from Sark where they had stopped off a little too long for a bathe in Derrible Bay. He wrote: '. . . The conditions for our passage to Alderney had not looked promising, and an hour after we left the weather worsened considerably. The distance from Sark to Alderney is only about eighteen miles but it took us longer than I had anticipated as the rising wind against the tide produced a steep sea which reduced our progress to about two knots. With Braye Harbour less than two miles away, the strong tide in the Swinge turned against us; we had visions of being swept miles off course, so we sailed into the shallows to try to cheat the tide but it was just as strong and we soon found ourselves drifting astern.

'With no suitable anchorage on the coast of Alderney (except Braye), we were in an unhappy position; I was gazing despairingly at the chart, when I noticed a solitary anchorage sign under which was printed "on S.W. stream"; according to the chart it seemed yachts could anchor safely just off Burhou Island. With relief, we sailed across the Swinge to our temporary anchorage with Burhou reef on one side and rocks on the other. This island, which is about half a mile long and one and a half cables wide, is deserted except for a refuge hut and thousands of puffins.

'At 2200 we weighed anchor and once more entered the Swinge. There was still a weak tide against us, but I was anxious to complete the passage without the assistance of the tide which, when it turned, would have made the Swinge very uncomfortable. The night was cold and black as we made our way across the channel. The sea was not rough but the occasional short steep wave broke against the side of the boat catching us unawares and drenching us with spray. The Braye transit lights seemed to take a very long time to come up, but in fact we were safely anchored in the harbour in time to hear the midnight forecast – moderate to fresh north-easterly winds; and so it was, blowing straight into Braye and giving us an uncomfortable night. But I daresay we should have been a great deal more uncomfortable had we remained anchored off Burhou. . . .'

Some years later, *Patsy* returned to Burhou. The large seas running in the Swinge, and a not insignificant tide, called for strong nerves to point the bows way up from the anchorage and we had hoped that, by good luck and judgement, having crossed the Swinge we should finish up off the narrow rock-strewn entrance. David and Richard stayed there long enough to scramble ashore to have a look at the refuge hut. I believe these days visitors are discouraged from landing on Burhou, particularly during the puffin breeding season as, sadly, their numbers have greatly declined.

On another occasion, David almost paid an unscheduled visit to Burhou, although I hasten to add that this was aboard another vessel. Prior to a Brittany cruise in *Patsy*, he had applied to Trinity House to visit the Casquets lighthouse to gather material for a couple of magazines who wanted articles on this group of rocks that stand in the western approaches to the English Channel.

The Casquets lie five miles to the west of Alderney, and Trinity House had arranged for David to be taken out on a regular trip to the lighthouse keepers in the motor vessel *Burhou* which was moored in Braye. It turned into quite a day out. *Burhou*'s skipper, Nick Allen, was also local pilot, Alderney Senator and part-owner of the local Seaview Hotel which was particularly hospitable to the crews of visiting yachts. The Allen family and friends which, with *Patsy*'s crew, made up quite a party, assembled aboard *Burhou* on a fine sunny afternoon.

Nick Allen anchored off Casquets where the tender was lowered. David, with all his camera equipment, was ferried to the sheltered landing place where one of the keepers was waiting with a rope which was the only means of scrambling up the face of the rock to the steps leading to a number of whitewashed buildings that make up this Trinity House station. There are three towers (on which beacons were lit before the introduction of lights), and a tiny 'terrace' which houses the keepers and the generating equipment.

David had clear instructions that when the foghorn was sounded, the shore party must return immediately. The visit went well and the keepers were pleased to receive a bundle of newspapers and magazines and some fresh food. They assembled at the landing to wave goodbye as *Burhou* weighed anchor and motored off in the direction of Alderney. About a mile off Braye harbour, the engine failed. While her crew struggled to restart it, the vessel was drifting closer and closer to the jagged Burhou reef which in years gone by has claimed so much shipping. Nick Allen hoisted the tiny steadying sail and, with great expertise, used tide and wind in an attempt to keep out of danger. Happily, the crew of a fishing boat in Braye had seen their plight and, to everyone's relief, came out to take the stricken vessel in tow.

\* \* \*

The facilities at Braye Harbour are good, with long lines of white mooring buoys to accommodate visiting yachts. It can, however, be very unpleasant if the wind comes round to the NE and strengthens. In a gale from the north-west, although the anchorage is reasonably protected, the seas can break over Braye's harbour breakwater which is dramatically illustrated in a photograph in Eric Hiscock's splendid book *Cruising Under Sail*.

Years ago there were no visitors' moorings, but plenty of room to anchor. I remember that when we were there in 1962, the north-easterly wind, in the late evening, had risen to gale force. We put out a second anchor, as did most of our neighbours; but nearly all the boats started to drag! There were shouts and screams; every yacht was lit up and two men in a dinghy were blown ashore unable to get back to their boat against the wind. Fortunately, our anchors held, but one of us had to stay up on anchor-watch as the turmoil around us continued throughout the night.

The wind had abated next day. Having decided to set sail for home, we attempted unsuccessfully to hoist the main anchor. The crew of a nearby ketch came over to give us a hand, but all to no avail. Using their powerful winch, they put so much tension on our anchor chain that some of the links were pulled out of shape!

I rowed over to the harbour master's office and explained our difficulty.

'Oh,' he said, 'you are foul of the big cable!'

Apparently, this was something which happened quite often. 'Don't worry,' he said, 'put a marker buoy on your chain, and cast it off. In due course we'll recover it.'

'But how do I get back my chain and anchor?' I enquired.

He assured me that the chain would be put on the deck of the next yacht leaving for Chichester. And so it was. About three weeks later Mr. R. M. Bowker of Bowker & Budd at Bosham telephoned to say that my anchor and chain were at his office and would I like to collect them?

## SARK

Because it is the nearest of the Channel Islands to the south coast, Alderney is the most visited by *Patsy*, and over the years has become a firm favourite; but

DROPPING ANCHOR IN THE HARBOUR OF CREUX, SARK

some of the family might vote for Sark, 16 miles to the south. It is quite different from Alderney, relying a great deal more on the tourist industry.

David and Richard remember vividly the contrast between the two islands when they were cruising towards St. Malo very early in the season. It was almost midnight as they approached Alderney, making for the Braye anchorage. Almost unheard of in the Channel Islands, it was actually sleeting. To make matters worse, *Patsy*'s carburettor was blocked, and the engine could only be used in short bursts by continually hand-feeding petrol into the carburettor chamber. They were so tired and cold when they got into port, that they simply removed their seaboots and turned in, knowing that they had to be up again at six in the morning to take the Alderney Race down to Sark.

They arrived there around eleven. The sun came out as they climbed the steep hill up from the harbour to the centre of the island. Memories of a few hours earlier of struggling into Braye were quickly dispelled as layer upon layer of clothing was discarded until they were soaking in the sunshine in their shirtsleeves. Spring flowers were everywhere, with the air full of birdsong.

David wrote in an article published in *Yachting Monthly* in January 1988 about the first time two of my grandchildren experienced the particular magic of Sark: '. . . We were on passage between Alderney and St. Peter Port, when I realised that conditions were ideal for Sark, if only we could make it before dark.

'The 1750 forecast had suggested the settled weather was continuing, and a double check on the tides confirmed we had an opportunity too good to miss. So, sweeping round to the south-east, we cut the corner, taking the Passe Percée between Herm and Jethou, heading for Sark with an anxious eye astern on the setting sun.

'It was dusk as we slipped between the black lump of l'Etac de Sark and Little Sark and then on past the riding lights twinkling in Dixcart and Derrible Bays, which looked particularly inviting anchorages on that summer's evening. With Creux Harbour half a mile away, and the Burons still visible off the entrance, we reckoned there would just be sufficient light for us to pick our way into harbour.

'Creux was packed with boats, leaving me bewildered as to what to do next, when the owner of the Westerly *Le Bonheur* invited us to lie alongside, pushing a couple of tenders out of the way to make room for *Patsy*. Someone under the quay lights was calling for our bow line and *Le Bonheur*'s owner kindly let us secure our stern line to his, which was attached to a firmly embedded stern anchor.

'After supper, as we put out the legs, the sound of an accordion drifted across the water from a French gaffer which was moored to dry out on the beach. Someone else then took over the entertainment from the harbour building on the quayside, which of all things houses a battered old piano. My children peered out into the darkness, curious to know where we were. They would have to wait until the morning to discover the delights of this postage stamp sized harbour, served by tunnels carved through the granite cliffs. . .'

Thirty years before my grandchildren's introduction to Sark, I remember an occasion when we had anchored *Patsy* off Creux because we had run out of drinking water. I rowed ashore, pulled the dinghy up on the beach and made my way to a point on the side of the cliff where I had been told that fresh water trickles out of a pipe. It was the most beautiful morning. The larks were singing and the seagulls calling as I waited for the jerry-cans to fill. Now, as everyone knows, there is a very high range of tide in the Channel Islands, and by the time the cans were full, the dinghy had floated off and had drifted over to the other side of the harbour! Fortunately, there was no-one about, so I stripped off my shorts, waded into the icy water, and swam, naked, across to the other side of the harbour and recovered the dinghy.

\* \* \*

There is a delightful stage play by William Douglas Home called *The Dame of Sark* which is based on Dame Sibyl Hathaway's autobiography. The play opened at the Playhouse Theatre, Oxford, with Celia Johnson playing the title role. The then Chairman of the Oxfordshire County Council decided to hold a reception to which the cast and the Dame of Sark were invited. Sadly, the Dame died before the opening, but her nephew, the new Seigneur of the island, and his wife attended, and were most impressed with the production.

Some years later, when Bill made it known in Oxford that we might be visiting Sark in *Patsy*, the Chairman of the County Council designed a splendid card for us to present to the Seigneur with his compliments. On our arrival, we anchored in Havre Gosselin to carry out our mission. It was a lovely morning as we climbed up the steep path from the anchorage, and made our way to the Seigneurie. The imposing iron gates were closed but we were able to open them and walk up to the grand house. A lady working in the garden looked at us rather askance as it was Sunday when visitors are not permitted (even to this day, the island rests on the Sabbath with no tripper boats running from Guernsey). But when we explained the purpose of our visit she told us that she was the Seigneur's wife and asked us in for a drink. Her husband, she said, was in the attic repairing the roof but he would be down in a minute. When he appeared, we had a pleasant chat, and then the two of them showed us round the Seigneurie including the Drawing Room of which the stage set at the Oxford Playhouse was an exact replica. In the play, which is about wartime occupation of the island, there is a dramatic confrontation between the Dame and the German Commandant. Standing there, on that Sunday morning, it was difficult to imagine that such things could have happened in such a peaceful place. When we left, three rather less famous names were inscribed in the Book of Distinguished Visitors!

A favourite novel, also set during the war in German-occupied Sark, is *Appointment with Venus*. The story, which was turned into an exciting and amusing film, is about a daring plan to capture a pedigree cow from the Germans. The British Force, with considerable difficulty, collected the animal (which the local Resistance had painted a different colour so as to disguise it), and made their getaway by sailing through the Gouliot Pass on the west side of the island. This is the narrow passage between the coastline and the island of Brecqhou, and the German gunboat patrolling the Sark waters was unable to follow the brave commandos with their prize cow.

I still get a thrill from sailing through the Gouliot Pass. It is only 70 metres wide, and the passage has to be timed with care because the tide hurtles through the channel at a reputed 10 knots. On either side are towering cliffs on the tops of which sit cormorants with outstretched wings waiting, one feels, like vultures, for boats to be dashed to pieces on the rocks below.

Sark itself is highly unusual. Local law forbids cars on the islands; but there are a few hard-worked tractors and an old power-driven vehicle on which the doctor makes his rounds. The boatloads of visitors can see the island by pony and trap or hire bicycles. Many make for Little Sark which is joined to the main island by La Coupé, said to be the highest and narrowest isthmus in the world. On the southernmost tip of Little Sark is Venus Pool, into which the fearless dive from the rocks high above. For me, however, it is in the evening when the last tripper boat has departed for Guernsey that the island becomes very special. Then only the locals and a few visitors are there to share its magic.

## GUERNSEY

A visit to Sark is wholly dependent on being in the vicinity in the right weather conditions. More often, we make use of neighbouring Guernsey as a passage port if we are bound for Brittany. When we first went to Guernsey in 1956, the inner harbour at St. Peter Port dried out. The man in the office on the pier head would shout out 'Anchor beyond the yellow buoy'. This was to leave sufficient room for the passenger ferries to turn. Since those days, a wall has been built across the entrance to the inner harbour and the outer harbour has been considerably developed. Yachts in their thousands, both English and French, call there either cramming into the inner harbour or rafting up to the visitors' buoys outside. I still find the town a delightful place to visit with its covered market, and its two hospitable yacht clubs, and I enjoy the climb up the hill to the Little Theatre.

In 1974 I sailed to Guernsey with Ken and Bill. We moored in the inner harbour at St. Peter Port, and lay alongside a French yacht whose skipper invited us to a drink aboard his lovely ship. He spoke good English and we had a very pleasant time during which we each consumed a few glasses of Pernod. After that we all trooped back to *Patsy* where we had a glass or two of white wine.

During the cruise, Ken, who is a good cook, had promised to serve us his famous *Sole Deauvillaise*, and where better than St. Peter Port? In the market one could buy not only fresh soles but also the famous Guernsey cream. *Sole Deauvillaise* is a dish highly to be recommended, but perhaps not before a sea passage. We had planned to leave for Jersey, catching the south-going tide which started around midnight, and were able to linger over the meal finishing with coffee and a spot of brandy. Having set sail with a fair wind, we reckoned we should reach Jersey before dawn. And so we did; but I spent most of the passage in my bunk. Avomine failed completely to stave off the effects of *Sole Deauvillaise* on top of Pernod. I witnessed *Patsy*'s departure from Guernsey about as far as St. Martin's Point; but then, like the man in Bret Harte's poem – 'the subsequent proceedings interested me no more.'

## HERM

Just off Guernsey, on the east side of the Great Russel, are two small islands Herm and Jethou. I have never landed on Jethou which is privately owned; but in 1957 we spent a marvellous weekend moored off Herm where visitors are made welcome and on which there is a splendid hotel.

At that time there were thirty-five inhabitants, presided over by Major Peter Woods and his wife, the tenants of the island, who invited us to their house. We attended a service in the local chapel and we explored the famous beach composed entirely of sea shells. There is a feeling about the island which it is difficult to describe. In Peter Woods's own words: 'Peace is not a negative thing – just absence of bustle and noise – peace is a positive thing, an almost tangible thing. On Herm there is peacefulness.' And so say all of us!

## JERSEY

The principal harbour of Jersey is St. Helier. We usually stop off there on our way to or from St. Malo. When we first visited the island, the facilities for yachts were very limited. The choice there lay between drying out in the inner harbour or remaining afloat alongside an oily pontoon in the entrance. Nowadays, like Guernsey, there is a large marina much used by visiting French and English yachts. My grandchildren have particularly enjoyed the island with visits to the vast entertainment complex reached by cable car high above the harbour or to Gerald Durrell's famous zoo for rare species.

Just two miles to the west of St. Helier is the drying harbour of St. Aubin where the headquarters of the Royal Channel Islands Yacht Club is situated. In 1974, we were invited to meet an old friend of Ken's who lives at St. Aubin and we thought it would be a pleasant change to berth there rather than in St. Helier. We had a fair wind, but it seemed prudent to enter the small harbour on the engine. All went well until we were about a hundred yards from the entrance when the engine packed up. Efforts to re-start failed, so we set the jib and sailed for the pierheads. When we arrived it became clear that the harbour was very crowded indeed; there was a rally of French yachts and there wasn't even enough space to turn! We hastily dropped the sail and threw out an anchor astern; but this manoeuvre was met by shouts of protests from the shore.

What was to to done? In vain we tried to coax the engine into life while the harbour master on shore became more and more excited. At last, one of the Frenchmen rowed across to us with a very long warp and towed us towards the moorings, while others took our warps and allowed us to lay alongside. Everyone (except the harbour master) was most friendly. That evening we dined in style with Ken's friend in the opulent surroundings of the Royal Channel Islands Yacht Club.

We sailed from St. Aubin to Gorey where we took the ground alongside the harbour wall; our surroundings in the shadows of Mont Orgeuil Castle were certainly picturesque, but the place was very crowded and life on board was nothing like as comfortable as a berth in a modern marina.

## LES ECRÉHOU

Six miles north-east of Gorey lies a group of tiny rocky islands called Les Ecréhou. I have never sailed there, but David has visited them and a picture of *Patsy* anchored off Marmotière appeared on the front cover of *Yachting Monthly*. He writes: '. . . Three of the islands have cottages on them, used by Jersey yachtsmen during the summer months only. Maître Île, the largest of the group, about 600 metres long, has the remains of a small chapel which belonged to the Norman Abbey of Val Richer, being granted to the Abbot on condition the monks kept a beacon burning, to warn shipping. The chapel was abandoned in 1415, and confiscated by the Crown, who have collected any rents from the islands ever since.

LES ECRÉHOU

'Marmotière, to the north of Maître Île, has its own slipway leading to a tightly-packed cluster of tiny cottages, some of which date back to the late seventeenth century. One of these buildings is designated the official Customs House, displaying the Jersey coat of arms and the inscription IMPÔTS. The cottages surround a square, affectionately known as "Royal Square", which is about the size of a table-tennis table. At high tide, almost all Marmotière is covered, leaving only a fistful of buildings, which at times appear to be moving at high speed through the water – a somewhat frightening optical illusion caused by the tide ripping through the Ecréhou. As the tide drops, the islands grow visibly until Marmotière is connected by a shingle beach to Blanche Île on which there are one or two more cottages.

'We landed on Marmotière's slipway, and climbed up the stone steps to the houses for a superb view of the rest of the rocks and islets that make up the Ecréhou. Then, as we walked over to Blanche Île, there was a hail from the skipper of a yacht that had been motoring up and down the Sound searching for mackerel. By the time we had strolled round Blanche Île, Peter Richardson with his crew Simon Airey were ashore, and taking us up to his father's splendid weekend retreat. As we paused in "Royal Square", who should appear from the shadows but Alphonse Le Gastolois – the recluse who, for 4 years, lived in highly publicised isolation on the rock, acting as caretaker of the houses in the absence of their owners, and operator of the radio telephone set – Ecréhou's one concession to the twentieth century.

'Alphonse Le Gastolois, one time Jersey fisherman, is reputed to have chosen isolation on the Ecréhou as a form of protest at having been publicly associated, quite mistakenly, with a series of horrendous crimes on Jersey. He spent both winters and summers on the Ecréhou, looking after the houses, and managing on an unbelievably spartan diet, supplemented only occasionally by any fish he could catch. While he was there, there was a mysterious burning to the ground of one house built on Maître Île. There followed a trip to the island by a party, including two vets, sent by the States Agricultural, to kill and capture some of the exceptionally large wild rabbits to make certain they were not rabies carriers. Alphonse, upset by the invasion, was carted back to the mainland to make an appearance in court. Although unanimously acquitted by a Jersey jury of 24 persons, Alphonse wintered in jail in comparative comfort and since that time has been only an occasional visitor to the islands. He fervently claimed they were his, and is reputed to have petitioned the Queen to be declared *"King of the Ecréhou"*.

'This fought-for kingdom must be desperately bleak in the winter months. In summer, however, Peter Richardson told us that the islands receive a fair number of visitors, mostly the crews of local boats or French yachts from the nearby harbours of Carteret, Portbail and Grandeville. On a fine weekend, the mooring off Marmotière can be packed with as many as six boats.

'Sitting in the bay window of Denys Richardson's Marmotière house, we studied a most interesting log which had recorded over many years everything that had gone on in the Ecréhou. *Patsy* lay quietly on the mooring just below us, with the sun dropping over the horizon at the end of another beautiful day. At dusk, under the expert direction of our hosts, we were able to motor *Patsy* straight into the "pool" half a cable WSW of Marmotière. Here we secured to one of the moorings while ashore a delicious supper was under way. We ate and drank well on Marmotière that night, while the high tide came and went. It was a curious sensation to be perched on the rock with the sound of waves lapping gently, just a few feet from the doorstep, leaving only the Marmotière cottages and flagstaff above water. In the early morning, we wished each other a good night, then we clambered into our dinghy, and set out on a long row towards *Patsy*'s welcoming riding light, bobbing just above the water in this fascinating anchorage. . . .'

## THE MINQUIERS

Further to the south, between Jersey and the French coast, lies the Plateau des Minquiers. Compared with Les Ecréhou, it covers a much larger area, amounting to about 80 square miles of rocks and reef at low water springs. Now used mainly at weekends, the little stone houses on the largest of the islands have long been registered as the property of the Jersey people. The Germans occupied Maîtresse Île during the last war, allowing only the French to fish these treacherous waters, and after the war France claimed the entire Plateau des Minquiers for herself. The past registration of the properties here was of great significance when the issue was taken to the International Court of Justice at The Hague, who ruled in favour of Jersey ownership. In spite of the decision, the French are still allowed by the British to fish here, and when Maîtresse Île was inhabited there were occasions when the Union Jack and the Tricolour flew together above this islet.

David writes: '. . . At low tide, the "Minkies" (as it is known locally) is a mixture of sandbanks, shingle and rocks, stretching as far as the eye can see and

HOISTING THE BRITTANY FLAG

occupying an area about the size of Jersey. Six hours later, only nine peaks remain uncovered, of which one used to be inhabited. This was Maîtresse Île which is about 300 metres long and where the original fishermen's cottages, built 200 years ago, still stand. One or two have been renovated and are used as weekend retreats by their Jersey owners or sometimes let for summer use. When we were there we were met by a family, including two small children, who were starting their fourth solitary week on the Minquiers. A disused Customs House here bears the Jersey Coat of Arms and there is a helicopter landing-pad (a joint English/French air/sea rescue venture). Although there is no fresh water or power supply, Maîtresse Île boasts of having the most southerly building in the British Isles – a fully operational loo which, from the outside, doubles as a seamark! . . .'

\* \* \*

I have never landed on the Minkies. Perhaps Hammond Innes's exciting novel, *Wreck of the Mary Deare*, which contains a vivid account of navigating in these waters, frightened me from doing so. I have, however, visited several times the Îles Chausey which lie 18 miles from Jersey and 7 miles from the Normandy coast. Although occupied by Jersey in the past, Chausey is very definitely French. It consists of one principal island, Grande Île, and innumerable small islets. Because of the huge local range of tide, the fascination of Chausey is the ever-changing scenery as the water drops rapidly away to reveal more and more of the archipelago. There is a deep Sound to the north of Grande Île in which moorings for visiting yachts have been laid, providing a useful place to wait during the period of adverse tide when on passage from Jersey to St. Malo. Grande Île has an hotel, a farm, post office and château. One day I would like to spend some time there, taking photographs and making sketches of the scenery.

## MARCOUF

Of all the islands in the English Channel, perhaps the most fascinating are the Marcouf, which lie 10 miles to the south of Barfleur and only 60 miles from the Isle of Wight. *Yachting Monthly* published an account of *Patsy*'s visit there which David titled 'The Umbrella Islands' – a reference to the need for some protection against the droppings of hundreds of seagulls that nest here. He writes: '. . . We set sail from St. Vaast-La-Hougue which is a small fishing port (nowadays it has a huge marina) just south of Barfleur. It was the end of a fine summer's day and a gentle breeze wafted *Patsy* towards the Île du Large and the Île de Terre which together form Les Îles St. Marcouf. On the largest scale Admiralty chart, these islands have the appearance of nothing more than two rocks with a flashing light on one of them. I had read in an article published in 1962 that, in the Napoleonic era, the two islands had formed a strategic link in the string of Normandy fortifications built to defend this vulnerable part of France from the British. Although uninhabited for many years, much remained of the fortress built by Napoleon on the Île du Large and it was evidently still possible to use the island's miniature walled harbour which dated back to the same period.

'As we approached, the great crumbling battlements on the fortress were clearly visible taking on a majestic golden colour in the evening sunlight. We soon picked out the red and white beacon marking the southern extremity of a drying shoal off the Île du Large that is one side of the narrow tide-ripped channel between the islands. A couple of cables beyond the beacon were two tiny spar marks in the entrance to the harbour. Once past the beacon, we were entirely dependent on a sketch map that accompanied the '62 article. Down came our sails and we moved ahead very cautiously on the engine. Opening up was what looked like the snuggest harbour imaginable.

'In my enthusiasm for our new found surroundings, my attention wavered from our directions, and I turned too soon for what I thought was the harbour entrance. Almost immediately *Patsy* grounded and seemed to be completely surrounded by small clumps of seaweed, attached to a rocky bottom covered by about 2ft of water. Fortunately, we had been moving very slowly, and with the assistance of the engine, we were able to pole off without much difficulty. I then jumped into the dinghy and, using an oar to take soundings, guided *Patsy* into the deeper water in the middle of the tiny harbour.

'It was after sunset when we finally dropped anchor. We were dismayed to discover that we had only 10ft of water below the keel. According to our information, there should have been a depth of 5ft at MLWS in the harbour, but with a tidal range of about 20ft at Barfleur, this just did not seem possible, since the ebb had barely started. We nervously weighed anchor and moved alongside the harbour wall, securing a head rope round the muzzle of an old cannon that had been sunk into the ground as a bollard. Above us, hundreds of gulls screamed in fury, resenting our intrusion and registering their protests most effectively! I made a mental note to put on the sail cover at the first opportunity; I thought too, that a visit to the Îles St. Marcouf should be made by that wag who said that the three most useless things on a yacht are a naval officer, a wheelbarrow, and an umbrella, for he would certainly discover a use for the last item.

'The great fortress loomed eerily over us, silhouetted against the night sky and lit at regular intervals by the flashing beacon. There was a remarkable stillness, broken only by the occasional cry from a gull and the ominous sound of water trickling out of the harbour. Examination with a pole revealed that the bottom beneath the boat was uneven, possibly due to fallen masonry and there seemed to be a ledge protruding at the base of the wall. It was obviously no place to dry out, so we moved again – back into the centre of the harbour. Two hours before low water we were still afloat, with a couple of feet of water below the keel. An hour later, at about one in the morning, we suddenly became aware that there was no longer the sound of water running out of the harbour. We rowed over to a rusty ladder and clambered ashore to investigate. In the moonlight, we could see quite clearly that the level of the water outside was much lower than the level in the harbour. It was a simple enough explanation as to why we were still afloat, and had I not been so ready to doubt our pilotage notes, we could have all turned in at a much more civilised hour.

'In spite of our late night, we rose early the next day for we wanted to explore the Île du Large before leaving on the next high tide. The gulls rose early too, screaming all around us, anxious that we might harm their young, whose nests were all over the island, often on open ground, and we had to be very careful to avoid treading on them. The baby gulls made pathetic attempts to hide from us amongst totally inadequate clumps of grass, or else they would stride out in front of us as fast as their tiny legs would carry them. It took us about 10 minutes to walk right round the island.

'The fortification must have been very effective in its time, for the battlements, with a liberal sprinkling of gun emplacements and magazines, are surrounded by a deep wide moat running right round the island, and it is only possible to enter the fortress through a passage from the harbour or by means of a rickety footbridge slung across the moat. Before Napoleon built the fortress, the Île du Large was occupied for a few years by men of the Royal Navy who harassed French ships sailing between Le Havre and Cherbourg. The battlements were finally abandoned in 1815, although the island was used for a short time during the last war by a German light flak unit. Later in the war, the Allies raided the islands preparatory to the D-Day landings, believing that heavy guns had been installed there  The raid was a terrible tragedy. The Marcoufs were deserted, but the beaches had been heavily mined and the raiding party suffered appalling losses.

'We left the harbour 2 hours before high water, setting sail for Grandcamps-les-Bains which is 8 miles to the south-east. From there we worked our way along the Normandy coast, nosing into some of the less frequented creeks and harbours, but of all the places we visited on that summer's cruise, those umbrella islands of St. Marcouf were certainly the most memorable. . .'

# CHAPTER 7

# BRITTANY

T HE discussions that go on in the family during the winter months, trying to decide where *Patsy* will spend the summer, are one of the
pleasures of cruising. Looking through three decades of logs, it is
interesting to note that half of our cruises have been to Brittany. Perhaps this
is not all that surprising as the North Brittany coastline is considerably nearer
to our home port of Chichester than Cornwall, Ireland, Holland or the Baltic.
The Channel Islands lie conveniently en route, and there is a ferry service between Portsmouth and St. Malo which is much used by *Patsy*'s changing
crews.

There are, of course, other attractions. We particularly like the Côte de
Granit Rose – a magnificent 40-mile stretch on the north coast between Paim-
pol and Trébeurden. It is the nearest part of Brittany to Guernsey, a distance
of 40 miles, and has many anchorages in wild scenery of towering rock formations. The north-west corner of Brittany, with its great Rade de Brest and
Baie de Douarnenez, is an area we have frequented more in latter years. But if
I were asked which, of all the cruising areas between Biscay and the Baltic, was

ST. MALO

my particular favourite, I think I would reply 'the west coast of Brittany'. The area between Benodet and the Loire is very attractive, and the locals claim that once south of the Pointe de Penmarch the weather becomes noticeably warmer and the sea a deeper shade of blue!

Several of our cruises have been restricted to the Channel Islands and the north coast of Brittany. This will usually include some time spent at St. Malo for which the family has a great affection. When we first went there, the port had no marinas or yacht basins. The Basin Vaubin was shared between commercial shipping and a handful of visiting yachts at the head of the basin, where each craft had its own mooring buoy and gang plank to the shore. Nowadays there must be over a thousand yachts here, but this in no way detracts from the charm of the place.

The old town was built on a small island of granite rock. The original thirteenth-century ramparts which encircled the island remain, but many of the buildings inside the walls were flattened in the last war. These have been painstakingly rebuilt almost exactly as they were, and many consider St. Malo to be the finest example in the world of post-war reconstruction.

We have enjoyed a number of holidays based on St. Malo; the area around the Rance estuary is particularly good for day sailing. It includes St. Servan and the Tour Solidor at which the story of *True as a Turtle* was filmed.

About 40 miles westward from St. Malo lies the Île de Bréhat. *Patsy* first put in there in 1957. Four years later she returned and her crew were astonished to discover picture postcards on sale showing her leaning up against the quay at Port Clos!

Making for Bréhat from St. Malo, it is well nigh impossible for *Patsy* to reach the island on one tide. We have, therefore, on a number of occasions stopped

THE TOUR SOLIDOR, ST. SERVAN

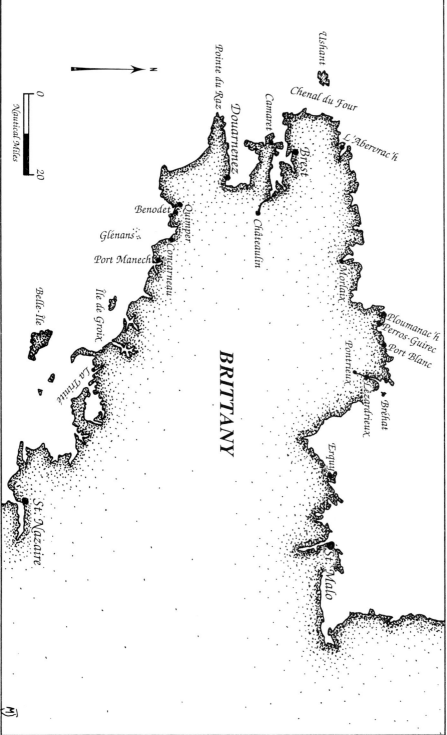

off at the small fishing port of Erquy for the period of adverse tide. The drying harbour is often crammed full of fishing boats; I remember on our first visit we managed to worm our way between the moored boats by rowing the dinghy through them, towing *Patsy* at the end of a very long warp, avoiding collision by fending off by hand! There happened to be a convenient space against the wall where we lay alongside and took the ground quite comfortably. On the far side of the road which runs parallel to the quay, just above where *Patsy* was lying, was a small bistro where we had an enjoyable drink or two in pleasant company; but unfortunately they kept open until very late, and the sounds of music and laughter in the small hours of the morning made sleep very difficult. Otherwise we passed a comfortable night. Our departure next day was much easier than our entry had been as most of the fishing boats had left.

In 1961 we arrived at Bréhat at low water and anchored just outside Port Clos. In the evening when the tide had risen, we motored gently into the harbour and lay alongside the stone jetty used for about two hours either side of high water by the vedettes which bring crowds of visitors to the island from the nearby Pointe de l'Arcouest; but by the time we had made fast the last of the tripper boats had left and it was all most peaceful. The moon came up and we slept soundly to the morning.

After breakfast, one of the locals hailed us and pointed out most politely that we were occupying the landing space used by vedettes which would be arriving at any moment; would we kindly move up the jetty into the shallower water? Naturally we complied at once and pulled *Patsy* further up the beach, mooring her against the wall. Then we walked into the village, had a drink and bought some postcards.

PORT CLOS, ÎLE DE BRÉHAT

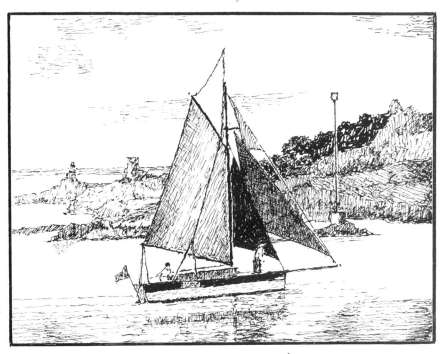

ENTERING LA CHAMBRE, BRÉHAT

Our party consisted of Doris and me, Richard (then aged 15) and brother-in-law John. We had another drink or two and wrote our postcards until it was time to walk back to the beach and haul *Patsy* back again into deeper water. When we arrived, one of the vedettes was unloading just below us and hoards of trippers were coming ashore. As the tide recedes at Port Clos, the vedettes move lower and lower down the quay for disembarking until there is insufficient depth of water when the operation is switched to another jetty much further down the harbour.

We waited patiently until the unloading was completed and the vedette had moved off. But alas, we had left it too late – *Patsy* was aground!

'Oh well,' I said, 'We'll stay here for the day and move down into the deeper water at midnight.'

'Monsieur,' said one of the locals, 'Do you realise that tonight the tide will be half a metre lower than it was this morning and that you will not be able to move?'

We were neaped!

'Well,' I said, 'if we had some help – a fishing boat perhaps – with a powerful engine, they could pull us off!'

'At midnight?' said our friend. 'Quite impossible.'

So we held a Council of War. We asked some fishermen if there was any hope of our getting her off at midnight, but they were all quite definite that there was no hope at all.

'You will be here for two weeks,' they said, 'but it is a pleasant place,

71

so rest content!'

Much as we all liked Bréhat, John and I both had to be back at our respective jobs before then, and the thought of spending a fortnight or more stuck high and dry at Port Clos filled us with dismay.

'Do you think there might be a chance of her being floated off at high water if we removed some of the ballast?' said John.

The ballast consists of wedge shaped pieces of cast-iron laid on concrete under the floor of the cabin. To remove them and lift them out on to the jetty would be an awful job, but we decided that it was our only hope.

We had some lunch and then set to work. It was very hot. The French fishermen looked on in amusement as we manhandled the oily lumps of ballast from the bilges, first on to the cabin floor, then on to the floor of the well and from there on to the jetty. It was back-breaking work, particularly for John who was prone to back problems. In addition, we removed every other heavy item from *Patsy* – the anchors and chain, the calor gas cylinders, the bunks, the watercarriers and even the stores of tinned food!

We borrowed a spade from the hotel overlooking the jetty, and dug a trench under the after end of the keel. Into this we laid some wooden planks which we found on shore. These we greased. I went to the fishermen again and persuaded them to lend us a heavy tackle.

'You waste your time,' they said.

One of the less pessimistic of the onlookers, after staring long and hard at our efforts gave a characteristic Gallic shrug and declared '*Une chance sur dix!*'

We made fast the tackle to a hole in *Patsy*'s keelson; and from another ring ashore we led our stoutest warp to the winch on the foredeck. Then we fastened the dinghy to the end of the boom, swung it out to starboard and hauled on the topping lift so that the boom was taking the weight of the dinghy. This, we thought, would help to heel the boat over to starboard thus reducing the draft.

We could do no more so we had a meal and nervously waited for the moment of truth around midnight. It was a beautiful evening, but there was not a soul about. We had worked out carefully from *Reeds Nautical Almanac* the precise time of high water and about ten minutes before zero hour we manned our stations: John on the winch on the foredeck; Doris and young Richard on the topping lift; myself on the fisherman's tackle leading from the stern. We all pulled like mad, but nothing happened!

The effect of the weight of the dinghy on the end of the boom resulted in some heeling, and by pulling the topping lift and then easing it we were able to cause a certain amount of rocking – but however much we pulled there was no movement at all sternwards. The stout warp to the winch on the foredeck was bar-taut and I thought that either it or the fitting on the deck might give way; but nothing happened.

Zero hour came and went. We were just about to give up when suddenly there was a slight tremor. We gave a shout and all pulled like mad! There was a sort of squelching sound as the boat moved sternwards an inch. After that it was relatively easy. Exhausted but elated, we pulled her back into deep water, replaced the bunks on board and turned in.

Next day we moved *Patsy* as far up the beach as we dared; but she was still quite a long way from the pile of ballast, chain, anchors etc. What was to be done? Some of the fishermen and a few of the local population looked on with interest. Among the latter was a small boy with a sort of wheel-barrow which he used for carrying visitors' luggage from the vedettes to the hotel. We gave him an enormous tip and persuaded him to lend us his barrow in which we ferried all *Patsy*'s gear from its pile on the quay. The fishermen, who had told us that to move the boat would be quite impossible, looked on indifferently as we stowed all the ballast. Not one of them came over and said, 'Well done!'

In 1962 young Richard wrote an account of this adventure which won the Dingle Cup of the Cruising Association.

\* \* \*

From Bréhat, we usually continue up the Trieux River to Lèzardrieux, which is perhaps the most popular of all the places on the north coast, offering a good marina and yacht club. It is possible to continue a further 7 miles upstream to the lock and town quays at Pontrieux. David first made this trip in 1957 when an English yacht moored there was something of a rarity, and *Patsy* and her crew attracted considerable interest from the local populace.

I myself have never been able to get to Pontrieux. The lock is just below the town, but on each occasion I have approached it, the lock-keeper has refused to open the gates to let us through. I gathered he would open up for sabliers and other commercial traffic, but not for yachts. David returned to Pontrieux in *Patsy* thirty years later, and had no difficulty in locking in. He reported that the place had been transformed. The sabliers had virtually disappeared and the quays are now lined with yachts for whom the authorities have provided good facilities. It was here that he found one of the most welcoming harbour masters on the entire north coast.

A few miles to the west of the Trieux is the Tréguier River which nowadays has a marina off Tréguier's quay. It was in 1978 that Ken, Bill and I sailed there, and on approaching the town we saw ahead of us a large vessel, junk rigged, very skilfully beating upstream and manned by a crew dressed as pirates! At the helm was Yvon Le Corre with whom we later made friends. We gave him a copy of David's book, *Brittany & Channel Islands Cruising Guide*, and in return he presented us with a most splendid volume of *Heureux qui comme IRIS* beautifully illustrated by Yvon himself.

Six miles to the west of Tréguier, David and Richard had what they claim to be one of their worst experiences aboard *Patsy*. David writes: ' . . . It was towards the end of what had been a splendid North Brittany cruise. Everything had gone like clockwork, and we had enjoyed lovely weather and great sailing. With two or three days remaining to work the boat eastwards towards St. Malo, we were enjoying a late afternoon off the Côte de Granit Rose. We were full of confidence, and decided it would be fun to put into the little harbour of Port Blanc for the night. We had not been there before; but we were undeterred by the difficult rocky entrance or by a mention on the forecast that the wind was swinging round to the North-West.

'Port Blanc is a tiny natural harbour. A yacht has to sail close inshore to find the harbour entrance which is a narrow gap between huge rock formations. The difficulty is that one gap in the rocks here looks very much like another, and most of the lighthouse on the high ground behind the harbour is often obscured by trees. On that occasion it was made the harder to locate by being viewed against the setting sun. Eventually we found the right gap and motored in, anchoring in total isolation. There is a small village ashore, but a good, popular restaurant where we dined that evening. On returning to the beach, we were conscious of a stiff onshore breeze, as we got a soaking attempting to launch the dinghy.

'I don't think either of us slept much that night as the rolling and pitching became worse. We took it in turns to go outside and peer into the darkness to see if the towering rocks that surrounded us were still in the same place. At about 8 o'clock in the morning when we were both in our bunks, there was a loud crack! We shot out of bed as Richard yelled that the anchor chain must have parted. He rushed up on deck while I hurled off the engine cover and went through the start routine on the old Stuart Turner at breakneck speed, fearful that in a matter of seconds *Patsy* would either be beached or dashed up against the rocks. Our prayers were answered and it started first flick of the handle.

'Richard yelled that he was going to try to get out of the harbour, but when we got to the narrow entrance, we met the full force of the wind and huge waves.

'"We're not going to make it," he shouted, "hang on, I'm going to try to turn!"

'With our hearts in our mouths, the wind pushed at the bows until *Patsy* was broadside on to the seas and we were fearful that we would either lose steerage way or be swamped. She rolled sickeningly, but then slowly came round and we were able to head back into the comparative safety of the harbour. When we had arrived the previous evening, we had examined a solitary mooring, but found that there was no chain to secure to, just a light piece of rope that went from the buoy down to the seabed. Having lost our anchor, we decided to use the mooring and if that parted we would have to remain underway on the engine inside the harbour until the weather improved.

'We were at Port Blanc for another 24 hours. Sick with worry and confined to the boat, it was misery. One of us would keep a watch outside while the other lay in his bunk, waiting for something to happen. We hardly ate, or read or listened to the radio, unable to relax until we had extricated ourselves from our awful situation. We were certainly paying the price for over-confidence! Every couple of hours or so, one of us would don oilskins and crawl up to the bows to move the mooring rope a few inches to prevent excessive chafe.

'By dawn next day, the wind had abated a little. A fishing boat went out so we hastily let go our mooring and motored after her. The surge of relief as we cleared the entrance was enormous. We were at last able to unwind in the sunshine, completing the sixty-mile passage to St. Malo in daylight.

'While we were at Port Blanc, we both ruefully contemplated that if we had not been so impulsive, we would have logically made for the security of Perros-Guirec, just five miles back down the coast. We could have spent a night or two safely tucked into the modern marina here and enjoying this holiday resort's night spots instead of miserably riding out the weather at Port Blanc. . .'

I have visited Perros-Guirec on many occasions. When I first went there it was a small drying fishing port; but like so many of the harbours along the north coast, the fleet has today almost disappeared and a retaining wall has been built across the entrance to the old harbour to form the marina. A similar transformation has taken place a little further along the coast at Ploumanac'h, which has, in recent years, become a firm favourite with the family. One look at a chart of the Côte de Granit Rose puts most people off even approaching Ploumanac'h, and for many years before the building of the sill, we steered well clear of this small drying harbour, with its dramatically rock-encumbered entrance.

*Patsy*'s first visit there was as a result of a chance meeting in Creux Harbour, Sark with Denis Le Bras, the owner of a beautiful French Old Gaffer. He rowed over to *Patsy* with a cordial invitation to participate in a *Grande Fête Maritime* to be held in 1987 at Ploumanac'h. He told *Patsy*'s crew that this was a very special event organised every four years for traditional sailing craft. Denis, who kept his boat there, was one of the chief organisers of the Festival.

When Richard was cruising with his young family along the north coast, and had put in at Perros-Guirec, he remembered that Denis lived locally and invited him to visit *Patsy*. They arranged that the following day, Denis would pilot *Patsy* along the coast and into Ploumanac'h. They were enchanted with the place, which has a magnificent château built on a tiny island in the rocky entrance. The story has, however, a sad ending. The yacht harbour had only recently been completed, and Denis's gaffer *Biskoaz Kemend All* was moored right at the edge of an area which had been dredged. The skipper had put out

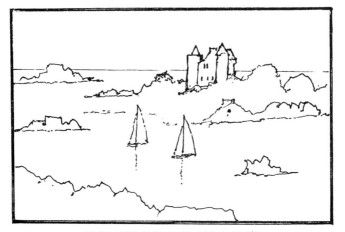

THE HARBOUR AT PLOUMANAC'H

legs but as the water level dropped, one leg took the ground while the other did not, and she started to heel over. Denis did not realise what was happening until too late. *Patsy*'s crew watched horrified as the hull slowly toppled over and lay on her beam ends, suffering considerable damage. A few hours later, Denis with a party of helpers, including a tractor on the shore which assisted in pulling her upright, managed to refloat her and move her into deeper water. *Biskoaz Kemend All* was later put on the market, and Denis started to build a magnificent replica of a *tonnier* or tunneyman, which was completed in time to take part in the 1987 Festival.

Leaving the Côte de Granit Rose, it is usually a six-hour passage on one tide to the popular sailing centre around the Morlaix estuary. On two occasions, I have sailed up the river and passed through the lock into the basin which is almost in the middle of the town itself. It was, I think, in 1970 that the Cruising Association H.L.R., Dr. Regis Pillet, walked over from his house to make our acquaintance as he did with every visiting English yacht.

Next morning, when we were preparing to make our departure at high tide, the skippers of two other yachts moored in the basin came over and said that the lock-keeper had gone on strike, and no-one knew when the gates would open. What was to be done? After some discussion, I made my way to the doctor's surgery. The receptionist took one look at my shabby sailing clothes and said that *monsieur le médecin* was engaged; but I told her the matter was urgent and I was eventually allowed to see the doctor himself and to tell him of our trouble. He said I should leave it to him and in about half an hour he came down to the lock and informed us that the gates would open immediately which they did. Long live the Cruising Association!

To the west of Morlaix is L'Abervrac'h the last of the sailing harbours on the north coast. There is a modest marina here and a delightfully secluded anchorage a further two miles upriver at Paluden. L'Abervrac'h is little more than a small village, but because of its position as the port of arrival/departure for West Country boats, the place used to have arrangements for supplying yachts with bonded stores. How different it all was compared with Cherbourg today where duty-free drink and cigarettes are simply collected over the counter. At L'Abervrac'h, one made one's way to the Bellevue Hotel to pick up an order form. This was taken, along with the ship's papers, to the Douane, conveniently situated next door. After about fifteen minutes the Douanier had to be revisited to collect the bill which was taken back to the hotel to be paid. The bonded stores were then issued against the receipted bills. Judging by the extreme reluctance of the Douanier when we were there in 1981, I reckon *Patsy* must have been one of the last yachts to take on bonded stores there.


## WEST BRITTANY

On one tide, even a modest sized craft can sail from L'Abervrac'h round the north-west corner of Brittany to Camaret or Morgat. This much-sailed passage between Ushant and the mainland through the Chenal du Four, misses out the

CAMARET

huge almost landlocked expanse of 40 square miles of water known as the Rade de Brest. A major port and anchorage for the French Navy, the Rade has a great deal to offer visiting yachts, and in recent years, we have made much more use of Brest, spending in 1985 one whole summer in and around these waters.

That year was typical of the way in which the family organises its holidays around *Patsy*. Richard cruised from Chichester to Morlaix. I then had to rush out to Morlaix with Ken and Bill a week earlier than planned because the yacht harbour was being closed for repairs and any craft remaining there would be trapped for several weeks! We sailed round the corner and into the Rade de Brest where we spent a few days, leaving her at Brest's Moulin-Blanc marina for David to take over with his children. He spent a fortnight in the Rade finishing up right inland at Châteaulin where he alerted the next crew (Colin and family) that there was to be a *Fête des Plaisanciers*. At the end of Colin's holiday, David returned with his cousin and a friend with just over a week to sail *Patsy* back to Chichester.

Colin decided to stay on at Châteaulin for the *Fête*, and while he was there he was approached by a representative of the local press. In the paper next day appeared: '*A bord du Patsy un petit voilier en bois, age 70 ans, ils ont sillonné, au gré du vent, la Manche, puis l'Atlantique. Ce n'est pas encore demain que l'on verra ce jou-jou rejoindre les cimetières de bateaux. . . Nous leur souhaitons tous bon vent!*' Along with the report was a photograph of Colin and Judith posing in the cockpit, and describing them as '*Vieux loups de mer*'!

David recalls making for Châteaulin up the Aulne river in which they stopped off for the night amongst a few boats moored there. It was impossible to escape the strong tide in the river where they had picked up a rather

COLIN AND JUDITH AT AULNE IN THE RADE DE BREST
*'Vieux loups de mer'*

insubstantial mooring. *Patsy* surged and swung so alarmingly that he decided to let go the buoy and to anchor a little more out of the tide. After a moderately peaceful night, they prepared to move on 14 miles up the river to the lock just below Port Launay. Nothing would shift the anchor which was well and truly fouled. The owner and crew of a Nicholson 34 came over to assist, and every text-book manoeuvre was attempted, but all to no avail. The Nicholson was well equipped, and her seamanlike crew produced a cold chisel and, having buoyed the chain, freed *Patsy* from her mooring.

Although the Nicholson had made previous visits to the Rade de Brest, her owner had not ventured further up the Aulne than the achorage. As the weather was unsettled, David suggested going up river in convoy to spend the night lying off the town quay at Port Launay, moored safely beyond the lock. That evening, both crews squeezed into *Patsy*'s tiny cabin to return the hospitality offered earlier in the Nicholson's spacious accommodation.

A day or so later, with David's holiday coming to an end, he thought he would make a last attempt to recover the anchor at low water. It was a wet, blustery day. They arrived at Trégarvan, up river of the anchorage, where they picked up a buoy and then huddled in the cabin with about two hours to wait. The youngest member of the family, Toby, happened to be looking out of the porthole and drew his father's attention to a huge rigid hull inflatable tender with several people aboard, some of whom were wearing wetsuits. David and Toby quickly launched *Patsy*'s dinghy and paddled furiously in their direction. They caught up with them ashore, loading their gear into a large truck. David explained his problem and the leader of the group said that they were off to the coast to waterski, but they would return at 5.30, and with that they drove off.

*Patsy* stayed on at Trégarvan. Low water came and went. From about 4 o'clock onwards, Toby scanned the shore for the return of the frogmen. 5 o'clock passed, and then 5.30. David was becoming a bit dispirited, when there was cry from Toby, 'They're back!'.

And so they were, their craft surging through the water at high speed towards *Patsy*. David and Toby jumped aboard and hung on as they raced down river at about 20 knots. They soon found the fender which was serving as the anchor buoy, and then the two who were going over the side went carefully through an elaborate safety check of all their equipment. They seemed to be down for ages. Eventually one of them appeared and conversed with their leader. David tried to read the expressions on their faces which looked distinctly pessimistic. The frogman then went down again to join his colleague.

The minutes ticked by. But suddenly a head emerged by the side of the boat, and David was asked to pull on the rope with the fender on the end. The chain then appeared together with the first frogman who was holding the anchor. There were cheers from *Patsy*'s crew – evidently working down on the river bed had not been easy because of the strong current and murky water. David tried to offer them a bottle of whisky for their troubles, but they did not drink and would not even take money for the petrol consumed. So it was handshakes all round and then they zoomed off back to shore at Trégarvan. David and his crew, elated by the success of their mission, proceeded back up river to the shelter of Port Launay, oblivious that it was by then blowing a full gale and raining very heavily.

As mentioned earlier, many yachts bound for the west coast of Brittany and sailing round from the north coast, give the Rade de Brest a miss, preferring the passage harbours of Morgat or Camaret. Of the two, I prefer Camaret. On our first visit there in 1961, the harbour was filled with langoustiers, strange-looking fishing boats which were constructed locally on the beach. They had a kind of hut on their deck through which projected what looked like a chimney stack. They sailed as far as Africa in search of their catch, and I think that these deckhouses may have been used for smoking the fish *en passage*. Alas, when we called there in 1985 there was none of these craft to be seen except for some derelict hulls drawn up on the beach.

There are now two yacht harbours at Camaret, and although the fishing fleet has disappeared, tourists in their hundreds pour into this busy town with its drying harbour, where every other quayside building is either a bar or a restaurant. By the main yacht harbour is a splendid Vauban Tower built as a memorial to the French Admiral who secured a resounding victory over a fleet of English and Dutch warships which had set out to invade that part of the coast. Now the base of the tower is used as a shower block for the crews of visiting yachts!

South of Camaret is the bay of Douarnenez. In 1963, David wrote in the December issue of *The Yachtsman*: 'We were at Douarnenez for the July 14th celebrations and more important (certainly as far as the locals were concerned) the *Fête des Mouettes* – the annual Festival of the Seagulls. Bastille Day seemed to be greeted with remarkably little enthusiasm. Towards late afternoon some flags appeared and some of the famous blue fishing nets were draped across the narrow streets; but I got the impression that these were only preparations for the *Fête des Mouettes* next day. In the evening we had a preview of the folk dancing and music which are big attractions at these local Breton festivals. Amateur groups of *cercles* and *bagads* take part. The *cercles* are the dancers and the *bagads* are the groups of musicians with bagpipes, drums and a rustic type of oboe.

'Later in the evening things really started to warm up with a Grand Bal which took place in a large hall above the fish market. This was a hot, noisy, colourful affair, during which the young people of Douarnenez proved that they were quite inexhaustible. The most popular were dances like the Conga and an energetic version of some dance that bore a slight resemblance to the Dashing White Sergeant, in which everyone stamped and cheered wildly around the hall. Some of the girls looked attractively beatnik dressed in yellow oilskin jackets!

'July 15th, and we had been at Douarnenez almost a week. By eight o'clock in the morning people were already lining the streets to await the grand procession which begins the *Fête des Mouettes* celebrations. This was an impressive affair, with floats of every variety, led by the local brass band who played their somewhat limited repertoire with great gusto. There were also a number of *bagads* in the procession looking very smart in the traditional Breton dress as they proudly marched to the skirl of bagpipes and crash of drums. Between the *bagads* came the local beauty queens – mainly blue-eyed, fair-haired girls with marvellous complexions. They wore sashes showing the region they represented over their traditional gowns. And, as always, there was a young visitor to Douarnenez riding a plodding cart-horse in the procession, who had the impressive title of Duchess of the Bretons and of Paris.

'The *bagads* and *cercles* performed all afternoon and most of the evening on a special stage that had been erected by the harbour's edge. It was as we were standing watching the folk dancing that we first noticed that the wind was no longer from the south-west. The flags and bunting surrounding the stage definitely showed signs of a little north in the wind. For almost seven days we had listened to every shipping forecast and gazed unhappily at the burgee, waiting for this northerly breeze. Every day we studied the tides and worked out a sailing time to arrive at the Pointe du Raz just before the west-going tide started to make. That evening we should have to slip just after midnight and miss the finale to the *Fête* which was the *Nuits des Mouettes*, another dance into the early hours of the morning.

'It was almost midnight when we returned to *Patsy* after watching an exciting firework display which had been organised by the local fire brigade! Standing in the cockpit, it was marvellous to feel a breeze from a different quarter, and BBC forecast confirmed the north-west wind for another 24 hours.

'So we slipped our mooring and the lights of Douarnenez soon disappeared astern. The wind was almost dead against us down the bay, so we motored into an uncomfortable swell with the sails up to steady us. We had been under way in this fashion for about three hours, when we sighted a sinister object in the water that was to accompany us for almost half an hour. There was no moon, and the bay was shrouded in darkness except for two flashing lights on the far shore. I assumed it was a boat, for all we could see (and there were two of us in the cockpit) was a strange black shape that was always in the same position – about 30 or 40 yards off our port bow. The uncanny thing about it was that there appeared to be no mast or sails, no sound of oars or engine, and no movement on the boat whatsoever.

'Then I heard bagpipes. I was on watch by myself this time, but unmistakeably in the middle of the Rade de Douarnenez, several miles off a bleak stretch of coastline, I swear I heard the skirl of bagpipes.

'The black shape disappeared with the first streaks of dawn. There was a big swell off the Pointe du Raz, but once round, the sun came up and we had breakfast and a wonderful sail down to the Anse de Benodet.

'The black shape of the previous night remained a mystery, and I was reluctant to mention the bagpipes. I had almost convinced myself that after the *Fête des Mouettes* I had bagpipes on the brain, or I was just over-tired, or that the noise of our engine was playing tricks with my imagination. It was not until we were safely anchored off Île Tudy that we discovered we had all separately heard the bagpipes!

'Since returning from the cruise, I carried out some research into the folklore of this part of Brittany and discovered that The Rade, under the ancient Celtic Menez-Hom (a hill overlooking the bay), was inhabited by ghosts, dwarfs, goblins, and the very unpleasant Ankou, the ancient figure of death! Ankou is a living reality to some of the Breton peasants. This personification of death appears either as a tall, haggard figure with long flowing white hair or as a skeleton with a revolving head so that no one can escape his fatal glance. He roams about with a creaking cart on to which he loads the corpses of those he has claimed.

'A little more research revealed that the bay held other mysteries. These waters cover the drowned city of Ys. Evidently, Ahes, the beautiful and lascivious daughter of one of the kings of this region, stole the keys to some sluice gates and gave them to her lover, who was the devil disguised as a handsome young man. He unlocked the gates, and let in the sea. The king and his daughter galloped for their lives on horseback in front of a vast tidal wave. The father escaped, but Ahes fell screaming into the turmoil. She now haunts the bay, luring fishermen down to the city of Ys. According to another legend, the souls of the dead are ferried across these waters to the Île de Sein which was at one time the haunt of Druidesses. And there are also numerous stories of dwarfs, gremlins and goblins. Dwarfs occasionally go to sea, for there is a reference to these people in the log of a cruise in 1952. On night passages, the skipper of the yacht had the company of a pleasant little fellow who would chatter away to himself quite happily up at the masthead while one of his less pleasant colleagues made a habit of creating a disturbance in the bilges!

'There is a possible explanation of our strange experiences. Instead of showing navigation lights, some of the local lobster boats occasionally stand a piper in the bows to warn other fishing boats of their presence. Even so, the memory of that dark night in the bay still sends a slight shiver down my spine. And having discovered about Ankou, Ahes and Ys, I think I shall be very reluctant to make another night passage in the Rade de Douarnenez!'

\* \* \*

After David's adventures in the Baie de Douarnenez in 1963, he sailed round to Benodet where he left *Patsy* for me.

They had been lucky to find a vacant mooring – it was before the marina had been provided there. Doris and I, my brother Arthur and Colin had crossed over to Cherbourg by ferry and had made the journey to Quimper by train and from there to Benodet by bus. It was a lovely day and Benodet was looking its best in the sparkling weather.

We found *Patsy*'s dinghy on the quayside and rowed out to her with our baggage. All was well. We had supper on board and turned in.

Next morning, Sunday, was fair with very little wind and patches of mist over the river. We therefore decided to proceed up the river to Quimper, on the engine, making the most of the last of the flooding tide. The engine started without trouble and we slipped the mooring.

The river Odet up to Quimper is very attractive; the channel is marked by withies. We were in high spirits on this the first day of our holiday; Arthur was at the helm and the rest of us on the foredeck when we came to a part of the river where the channel appeared to fork. We should, of course, have gone into neutral and carefully surveyed the situation but Arthur, for some reason or other, was convinced that the channel followed the starboard fork and boldly headed in that direction. Of course we went aground. Again, if we had had more sense we would have waited for half an hour until the flooding tide would have floated us, but we were eager to get on so Arthur put the engine into reverse while the rest of us rocked the boat from side to side – and behold she started to move sternwards! No-one bothered about the tiller and after a few seconds there was an ominous crack! We hurriedly changed into forward gear and, to our horror, the bottom half of the rudder dropped off and sank gently to the bottom of the river!

Words fail me to express our feelings of disaster. We had had less than an hour's sailing on a fortnight's holiday and here we were completely out of action!

Disconsolately we motored into deeper water and dropped anchor. The sun came out and the mist disappeared; but it did not relieve our gloom. Eventually it was decided that Arthur and Colin should try to make their way to Quimper to enquire about getting a new rudder. I rowed them ashore, wished them good luck and returned to *Patsy*.

Hours passed. The level of the water in the river rose and then started to fall. After a while the reeds on the top of the bank on which we had run aground appeared above the surface of the water, so Doris and I rowed across and there, lying in the mud, was the bottom half of our rudder!

With some difficulty we dragged it into the dinghy and thence on to *Patsy*. Now what was to be done? There were still no signs of Arthur and Colin so we thought we would go and look for them. We rowed ashore, leaving *Patsy* at anchor, and a passing motorist kindly gave us a lift into Quimper.

To our astonishment the town was packed with people, many of them in national costume – or rather in the particular costume of their particular town or region. It was the festival of the Cornouaille and posters advertised the fact that here were assembled over a thousand bagpipes! The noise was deafening. We threaded our way along the picturesque street which runs by the side of the river and there sitting outside one of the cafés were Arthur and Colin drinking Pernod. It was evident that that was not their first! They said that they had made enquiries about a rudder, but as the whole population was *en fête*, no-one was interested. They had however been given the name and address of someone who might help.

By this time the procession had started and it certainly was an amazing spectacle – banners, bagpipes, white lace head-dresses of every description, black velvet skirts, embroidered aprons and the men dressed almost as gaily as toreadors! Fortunately just then the bagpipes were silent. I threaded my way to the address given us, but, of course, Monsieur was not at home. So we decided to return to *Patsy* and bring her up the river on the flooding tide – steering if possible with an oar. This manoeuvre we successfully accomplished, bringing *Patsy* up to a quay just short of the first bridge and from there we watched a most splendid display of fireworks and afterwards passed a fairly peaceful night.

Next day Monsieur came down to the boat and surveyed the damage. He said that he could mend the rudder by bolting iron straps across the two halves, so we carried them to his workshop a few streets away. The accident in

WAITING FOR THE RUDDER AT QUIMPER

the river had also broken the tiller, but we found a suitable piece of wood, Monsieur lent us the necessary tools and we made a new tiller which, though it did not look very smart, served its purpose most admirably. By mid-afternoon Monsieur had finished his repair and together we carried the rudder back to the boat. It was now low tide and *Patsy* was sitting in the mud, leaning against the wall. To step the repaired rudder was not going to be easy; but as we contemplated the situation, a troop of French boy scouts came by, headed by the scoutmaster. They paused and looked at *Patsy* with great interest. We explained to the Scoutmaster that our '*gouvernail a été cassé*' and that the problem was how to refix it, whereupon he pushed us to one side, ordered two of his scouts below into the mud, lashed a rope round the rudder and with several small boys on the foredeck guiding it, it was lowered into position before you could say Baden-Powell. I think they all enjoyed it – even the two who stood on the river bed and got very muddy in the process!

* * *

My last visit to Benodet was in 1988 when *Patsy*'s engine had broken down. We found a most helpful engineer who carried out the necessary repairs and we had a very pleasant couple of days moored in mid-stream in lovely weather. We were still using the same old rudder with its straps of iron fitted up river at Quimper twenty years ago!

Ten miles to the east of Benodet is Concarneau where yachts have a good marina in the shadows of La Ville Close which is a great Vauban fortification almost entirely surrounded by water. Here the great ramparts encircle their own miniature town of cobbled streets and old houses, mostly taken over by souvenir shops and art galleries. One can take a quiet stroll in the evening along the top of the ramparts, then explore the little streets below; or one can visit one of the excellent restaurants in the town proper. I like the place enormously, and was horrified to read of the devastation of the yacht harbour there by the hurricane of October 1987.

A few years before, Ken, Bill and I had sailed *Patsy* from Chichester, spending a fortnight working her round the Brittany coast to Concarneau. Here Ken and Bill left to return to England, and I was joined by David. Within a few minutes of his arrival, *Patsy* was visited by the Customs who looked at the Ship's Papers and discovered that our only entry into France was registered at Cherbourg. The Douanier soon established that from Cherbourg, we had sailed to the Channel Islands, and then re-entered France on the north Brittany coast where we had failed to clear Customs (the regulations are much less stringent today!).

Before David had even started his unpacking, I was being taken ashore in the customs launch for further questioning. I returned about an hour later, under strict instructions that *Patsy* was to remain in port. Poor David, he only had eight days holiday, and there we were, unable to go anywhere until the matter had been resolved. Happily, after a long wait, the Douanier returned to say that his superior was prepared to overlook my folly, and we were free to leave, but by then it was late afternoon.

We set out from Concarneau early the next morning, stopping off for a few hours at Port Manech which lies in the entrance to the river Aven, facing another river entrance, the Belon, which is famous for its oysters. This small holiday resort is a great favourite of mine. It has a sandy harbour which dries, but there are several visitors' buoys in the river just off the harbour entrance.

Port Manech is a splendid place to stay in fine weather. In 1974, we were a party of six; four of us stayed in the Hotel du Port, where we had a car at our disposal, and two lived aboard *Patsy*, moored opposite the hotel. On September 3rd, it was decided that Colin, Judith and Noel should sail round from there to Beg-Meil – a distance of only twelve miles – and that we should drive round to meet them. The morning was sunny with a moderate breeze.

After breakfast, they slipped their mooring and sailed out to sea, while we went inland by car to Pont Aven and visited a picture gallery which is associated with Gauguin. While we were there, the sky darkened and a fierce storm blew up with a very strong wind and a downpour of rain. We sheltered for a while at Pont Aven and then, still in a downpour, made our way to Beg-Meil; but when we got there, *Patsy* was nowhere to be seen! As I waited, two yachts came in from the south and I asked their wet and bedraggled crews if they had seen anything of a gaff-rigged cutter; they both replied 'no'; so I drove back to Port Manech where there was still no sign of Colin and the mooring was vacant.

By this time, I was very worried indeed, so I returned to the hotel at Beg-Meil in the hope that there might have been a telephone message; no call had been received. So then, still in the pouring rain and strong wind, I drove back to Concarneau on the off chance that they might have run for shelter in that direction. In vain I searched the harbour. More worried than ever, I drove back to the hotel at Port Manech. Yes, there had been a telephone call. *Patsy* was safe!

It appeared that Colin had sailed out of the harbour and into the open sea when the storm came on. Judith had become very seasick and, as the storm seemed to be getting worse, he had decided to put back to Port Manech; but the wind was blowing straight into the estuary and, as the Port Manech moorings were very exposed, he had decided to go on up river to Rosbras. When he arrived there and found a mooring, the wind was so strong that he had not been able to row the rubber dinghy to the shore in order to telephone, and that was why there had been no message until much later. That day (September 3rd 1974) was the day that Edward Heath's *Morning Cloud III* sank off Selsey due to a freak wave.

\* \* \*

Two years later, we were back again at Port Manech. John, Noel and I had a holiday there, sleeping in the hotel and day-sailing in *Patsy*. One morning, we sailed over to the Îles Glénan ten miles away. The Glénans are world famous because of the sailing school founded here in 1947 by ex-members of the war-time French Resistance. Together, the Glénans form an archipelago of nine tiny islands and numerous offlying rocks and shoals. Thre are several anchorages, and on one of the islands, Île Saint-Nicholas, there are fishermen's cottages, a small hotel and a couple of bars.

We had anchored off Île de Penfret, and rowed ashore to explore. It was pleasant weather – sunny with a light breeze. While we were there, an elegant yacht – like the Dragon-class in appearance – sailed in and dropped anchor near to us. The owner spoke good English, and said complimentary things about *Patsy*. He asked us where we were staying, and we told him we were at Port Manech. He said that he owned a house there, overlooking the river. We bathed, had tea and then waved goodbye and sailed gently back to our mooring opposite the hotel. About an hour later, there was a knock on our topsides. Our friend had come to say that there was a gale warning and that we would find it very uncomfortable moored for the night where we were. He suggested we should move upstream and that he would point out to us where best to anchor. This he would do by signals from the balcony of his house. He had motored down from there and then rowed out to us to give us this warning!

Needless to say, we promptly followed his advice and when we arrived opposite his delightful house, there he was on the balcony, waving to us to drop anchor at a point where the water was deepest. Later on, he invited us over for drinks and suggested that we could make use of his private jetty while *Patsy* lay at anchor in that part of the river.

I shall never cease to be amazed at the kindness, help and hospitality which we have received from complete strangers when we have visited Brittany. I would very much hope that French crews putting into Chichester Harbour would receive from us as much neighbourliness as we have experienced over there, but I think this is most unlikely! I wonder why? Is it shyness or just indifference?

I will quote another example of some of the marvellous Breton hospitality we have received over the years. I have mentioned earlier that I had arrived at Port Manech with David, having sailed there from Concarneau where I had been detained by the Customs. We then sailed on to the Île de Groix where we spent the night. There is an inner harbour here with a sill built across the entrance. It is small and gets very crowded, but there is nearly always room in the outer harbour, part of which is well sheltered. Four miles long and about a mile wide, Groix is rather a bleak island, and we use it mainly as a passage harbour, rarely getting further inland than the first bar.

Belle-Île, like Île de Groix, is also much used as a passage harbour by yachts cruising up or down the Bay, but beyond this any similarity ends. About ten miles long and five miles at its widest, Belle-Île really lives up to its name. The big attraction of the place is the contrast in anchorages. There is Le Palais, which is crowded with boats and with plenty of activity and nightlife ashore; Sauzon, a drying fishing port with quays overlooked by pastel-coloured houses; and there is Ster Wen, which is a deep fjord on the island's Côte Sauvage and perhaps the most dramatic anchorage we have found anywhere in Brittany.

We sailed the thirty miles from Île de Groix to Belle-Île in about six hours, picking up a mooring off Sauzon. Although Belle-Île has in recent years become very popular with the family, on that occasion our enjoyment was marred by the engine refusing to start when we wanted to leave. After trying for over an hour, we gave up and hoisted sail. We had sought advice from people moored nearby who suggested that we would be more likely to find a mechanic at Le Palais.

The outer harbour at Le Palais was very crowded and it was extremely awkward not having an engine; but we managed to manoeuvre ourselves onto a large mooring buoy in the centre of the harbour. We went ashore in search of a mechanic, but as it was Saturday afternoon, none was available. Again we asked advice and were told that we should stand a much better chance over on the mainland at La Trinité, which is a major yachting centre. Here we would certainly find someone to look at our engine, although we would now almost certainly have to wait until the Monday.

La Trinité lies on the west side of the Crec'h river, which is packed with moorings and two marinas, the upstream one catering for visiting yachts. As we approached the Crec'h entrance, we were overhauled by a French yacht whose skipper offered assistance, piloting us towards the first of the marinas and a private berth near the yacht club. Her crew leapt ashore before us to fend off and take our lines.

While we had been sailing up the Crec'h, a friend of the French crew had been giving an hilarious demonstration (mostly in the water) of his athletic prowess with a windsurfer. We invited the French crew aboard for drinks and were soon joined by the intrepid windsurfer who turned out to be a wizard with engines, and within an hour had tracked down an electrical fault by turning over the engine and giving himself mild shocks from the battery.

That evening found us dining ashore as guests of these hospitable people in their stone cottage, with a roaring log fire in the middle of a room filled with the sounds of Breton songs and music.

To the south and west of the Quiberon peninsula lies the Gulf of Morbihan. This is a most interesting area in which to sail a small boat. They say it consists of at least three hundred islands, though some of these are not much more than isolated rocks.

In 1974 at a restaurant in Auray we met the owner of one of these islands who told us that it was unoccupied for most of the summer and that we were welcome to land there. We took him at his word and had a picnic on the beach there and swam in lovely surroundings.

The Morbihan is a very pleasant place to visit; but one must be wary of the fierce tides, especially at the entrance. I could write more about our visits there, which were delightful; but we did not experience any adventures which are worth recording.

# CHAPTER 8

# IRELAND

I N 1967 we set out from Chichester Harbour bound for Ireland. David sailed with me as far as St. Mawes, and it was on this West Country leg of the cruise that we gleaned some more information about *Patsy*'s origins. We had worked her up the coast to Newton Ferrers on the River Yealm, and from this delightful anchorage we had made an early start for Fowey, about 24 miles further on.

Around lunchtime, we found ourselves off the little fishing harbour of Polperro, and, as it was high water and we were not pressed for time, we made one of those spur of the moment decisions to call in. After we had secured alongside the old quay, we were warmly welcomed ashore by Jack Jolliff, Polperro's harbour master. He was joined by some of his fishermen colleagues who all eyed *Patsy* with great interest. Jack Jolliff announced that

'Either the *Phyllis* or the *Lloyd George?*'

she was undoubtedly a Polperro Gaffer. After a brief inspection, the locals reckoned that she was originally the *Phyllis* or possibly the *Lloyd George*. This new information led David on an interesting trail of clues, an account of which was published in 1977 in *Small Boat* and is reproduced in the Appendix.

When David left at the end of the week, I was joined by Dick Tomsett, and together we sailed without any special adventures to Newlyn, which is 160 miles from Waterford in southern Ireland. With a forecast of winds from SW to W, 2–4 increasing 4–5, I was in some doubt as to whether or not to set out. Dick, however, seemed keen to go so we slipped at 11.30, to make the Irish Sea crossing. By the time we got to Land's End, the visibility had worsened considerably and the wind had freshened from the west. Conditions were most unpleasant and, to make matters worse, Dick had become seasick and had retired below!

I felt that, under the circumstances, it would have been foolish to proceed on the passage to Ireland, so I turned *Patsy* northwards and then north-eastwards to run along the north coast of Cornwall – an area which we had never visited before. The visibility was getting worse and, after a while, through the fog I heard a siren sounding one blast every 15 seconds. I examined the chart and consulted Reeds but could find no reference to iden-tify the sound. It was all very worrying, when suddenly, right ahead, appeared an enormous headland with waves breaking on the rocks below. I promptly gybed and shot out to sea to the alarm of poor Dick who was by then feeling like death.

After about an hour, the visibility improved and Dick was feeling a little better, so we went about, closing the shore until we could make out St. Ives. As the tide was low, we were unable to enter harbour, so we had to spend a most uncomfortable night, pitching and rolling in the swell, anchored in the lee of St. Ives Head. Next morning was warm and sunny, and we spent a most pleasant day, with *Patsy* dried out against the harbour wall.

Admiralty Chart No. 2649 only extends as far northwards as Tintagel Head and, as we had intended to sail direct to Waterford from the Lizard, I had no chart on board of the Bristol Channel, nor was I able to buy one in St. Ives! It therefore seemed prudent to sail on to Padstow where we were told a chart would be obtainable – and this we did.

Padstow is a pleasant place in which to moor and the weather was lovely; but, alas, no chart of the Bristol Channel was to be had! It seemed foolhardy to set out across the estuary – where the tides run fiercely – without any chart at all, so, after consultation with Dick, we laid the back of an old chart alongside Admiralty Chart No. 2649 and extended on to the blank sheet the lines of latitude and longitude. Then from Reeds I plotted the positions of the lights etc. on Lundy Island and on the coast of Wales and, with this makeshift chart, we set off across the estuary bound for Milford Haven about 65 miles away. By taking the bearings of the lighthouses on Lundy Island, we were able to plot our position and navigate safely on to Milford Haven, where we made our way up to the anchorage at Lawrenny and spent a most peaceful and plea-sant time there.

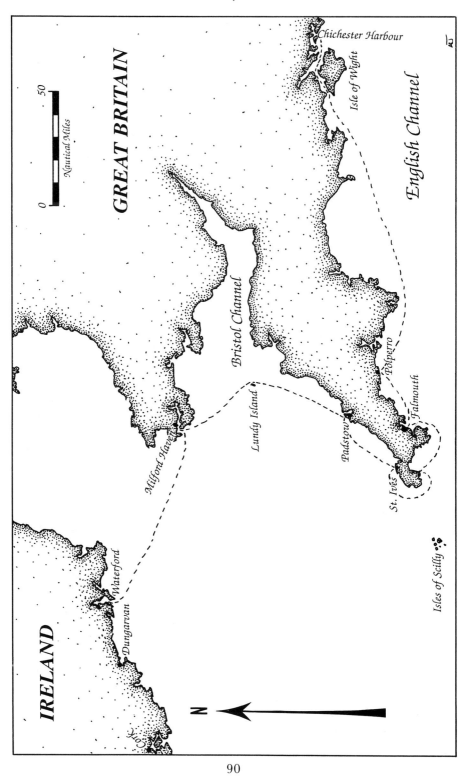

The passage across the Irish Sea to Dunmore East (about 120 miles) was uneventful. Instead of entering the harbour, we anchored off a little beach to the west where we were sheltered by the cliffs from the prevailing winds. The bathing was good here, and there was a path leading up to the town. We stayed there a couple of days, but then the wind went round to the east which made the anchorage uncomfortable; so we motored *Patsy* into the little harbour and dropped anchor. There was plenty of room. We were told that this is usually the case except during the herring fishing season when Dunmore East is often full to capacity.

Next morning, while we were having breakfast, a man came rowing across to us in a dinghy and said we had better move *Patsy* as they were going to start some blasting. We asked him when this would be, to which he replied: 'Sure, I don't know; t'will be some time yet tho', so finish yer breakfast, and a good day to you!' We returned to the cabin and had one mouthful of porridge when *Patsy* was nearly blown out of the water by an enormous explosion! They were blasting out the rocks at the bottom of the harbour quite close to where we were lying! So we promptly weighed anchor and started the engine to get away from the danger as soon as possible.

At that time, *Patsy*'s engine was an 8 hp Stuart Turner. It had been installed just after the last war and was therefore far from new. It had, of course, been overhauled from time to time, and gave us very good service indeed, particularly as I know nothing about engines. But I must admit that, on occasions, very rude things have been said about it by members of the crew, and this was such an occasion! As we made our way across the harbour, the gear lever stuck fast. In spite of our struggles, nothing would persuade it to return to neutral; so, there we were, going round in circles in Dunmore's small harbour to the astonishment of the people ashore. However, no damage was done, and eventually we managed to free the lever and to moor alongside an Irish Ministry of Fisheries trawler up against the wall.

The crew of the trawler said that they were leaving during the night, so we offered to move to another berth; but they said 'Don't bother – stay as y'are and we'll make ye fast whin we're off. An I suppose ye wouldn't say "no" to a crab or two?' They gave us several, which were delicious. Next morning we found ourselves lying up safely against the wall – they had set off during the night and we hadn't heard a sound!

Dick Tomsett returned home as his holiday was up and John Wiberg came out to join me. John, who likes his pint at the local, soon discovered the pub at Dunmore which turned out to be a grocer's shop with a bar at the back. We looked in one evening to find the only occupants were three locals who appeared to have been drinking for some time. One of them was sitting silently by himself at the end of the bar; the other two started talking to us.

We discussed the weather and world affairs in general; then they became anxious to know what we thought of Ireland, especially the North. We picked our way very gingerly through this minefield when, suddenly, one of them – a stout little red-faced man – drawing himself up to his full height of about five feet, said: 'D'ye know I'm one of 'em myself!' Then he paused, looked round and in a whisper added, 'There's a thousand quid on me head – dead or alive!' Whereupon John, who is a big fellow, grabbed him by the scruff of the neck and the seat of his pants and said, 'This is the easiest thousand pounds I've ever made!' We then bought him a drink and we were all pals. The conversation continued until the third man who had been sitting by himself without saying a word to anyone, slowly leant back and fell flat on the floor completely unconscious. No-one took any notice at all! But when our two friends started wrestling and throwing chairs about we thought it was time to leave.

It was Sunday at Dunmore East and a most beautiful day with a blue sky and a light wind. I ws told that there was to be dinghy racing, and quite a crowd had assembled on the pier; I ws surprised that the locals took so much interest in the sport. The five-minute gun was fired and the fleet started manoeuvring for the start when a small launch entered the harbour and drew up at the stone steps just below where I was standing. There was some commotion among the crowd and some cheering; but I took no notice as I was interested only in the dinghies. Suddenly a tough-looking fellow came up to me shaking his fist, 'And you had your back to herself when she passed!' he said so aggressively that I thought he might knock me into the sea. It appeared that Mrs. Jacqueline Kennedy, who was staying for a short holiday at a large country house near Dunmore East, had just landed on the quay; the crowd was there with one purpose only in mind and that was to welcome this celebrity. No-one gave a thought for the dinghies lining up for their race! Mrs. Kennedy had stopped for a cup of tea at one of the village shops where later we were shown the cup she had used which had been carefully wrapped in cellophane; for all I know, there it remains today, lovingly preserved in this fashion.

While we were in Dunmore East, we made an expedition to Waterford to see a production of J. M. Synge's *Playboy of the Western World*. This was performed by a talented bunch of local amateurs at the small theatre which I estimate had an audience capacity of about fifty. There were five or six shows each week, with the cast taking turns to play the parts. I have seen *The Playboy* many times, but I have never enjoyed a production so much as this one. It was so splendid to hear the lines spoken with an authentic accent. It may be that the accent was not really authentic and that there is a considerable difference between the dialects of East Waterford and Connemara, but it all sounded delightfully authentic to me.

At the fall of the curtain, the producer came forward and thanked his audience. He spotted us as strangers and kindly invited us to join him and the cast back-stage for what he said might be 'a cup of cocoa'. John, always out for a leg-pull, mentioned that at home I was a distiguished amateur actor, and this led them to ask my advice on forthcoming productions; but, alas, all my suggestions were for plays which involved the payment of royalties, and it appeared that their box-office income was so small that they were compelled to limit their shows to classics which were copyright free!

We returned home by ferry from Waterford, leaving *Patsy* at Dunmore East for Richard (who was at that time a law student) and Martin, a college friend. They were fortunate in having much of the long summer vacation to sail *Patsy* back from Ireland. This is Richard's account of their voyage: 'A lorry roared past, showering us both with muddy water. We had been standing on this desolate stretch of road between Portsmouth and Southampton for nearly three-quarters of an hour, and it was just beginning to rain again. We had both privately decided that the sensible thing would be to catch the next bus home, but neither would admit it, so we stayed, thumbing with ever-decreasing hope at the passing traffic.

'We were on our way from Chichester to Dunmore East, near Waterford where *Patsy* had been left for us. We had decided – or rather, I had decided, as Martin kept reminding me as we stood disconsolate in the rain – to save money by hitch-hiking to Fishguard instead of catching trains. So we had left home in the early morning hoping to make Fishguard by 0200 the next day which was when the ferry left for Rosslare. In fact, we made it in time to have a hot pie and a pint in the local pub before it closed at 2300 – our fastest "passage" of the holiday by a long way!

'After an uneventful ferry crossing, we caught the train to Waterford, having decided we had had enough of hitch-hiking. It then took us three hours to get to Dunmore East, a distance of about ten miles. We would have gladly caught a bus, but there seemed considerable doubt as to whether a bus would come. Our enquiries produced an amazing diversity of replies ranging from: "T'will be along shortly" to "The bus? . . . I'm not sure whether it's today or tomorrow" and we never did see one. We were in Ireland.

'It was with some relief that we finally arrived at Dunmore to find *Patsy* lying snugly against the harbour wall, looking very much at home surrounded by small fishing boats. We spent the remainder of the day exploring the village and sampling the national drink, discovering to our delight that licensing hours in this part of the world seemed virtually non-existent. The next day we went for a short brisk sail in Waterford Harbour to enable Martin to become familiar with the boat; but a forecast of a force 6 contrary wind and fog kept us in Dunmore for another day. That did not worry us as we were enchanted with the place and were already being affected by the atmosphere of inertia and lack of urgency that seems to envelop the land.

'Eventually we dragged ourselves away, for we had arranged a rendezvous with my brother, Colin, at Dungarvan, about 20 miles to the west. It turned out to be one of those passages which make one wonder why one spends one's time cruising instead of taking a proper holiday like everyone else. The forecast had seemed fine – wind southerly, 3 to 5, which would give us a good reach along the coast. We slipped at 0930, motored out of the harbour, and set a reefed mainsail. The wind was much more inclined to a force 5 than 3, and we were soon speeding along the coast; but the seas were most unpleasant, much rougher than we had anticipated. Martin became violently seasick and was soon oblivious to the world.

'Dungarvan is a small fishing harbour at the head of a natural estuary which, on the chart, looked easy enough to find in good conditions but not, as we were to discover, through a fine drizzle which was reducing visibility to little over a mile. It was an unenviable situation – half the crew incapacitated with seasickness, the other half feeling none too healthy, and the mist closing down on a totally unfamiliar coastline. After about four hours, we were immensely relieved when we identified through the gloom the lighthouse in the entrance. We rounded up in the calmer waters and cautiously moved forward on the engine. The sea mist became so thick that we were unable to make out the channel, and then the echo sounder revealed that the bottom was rapidly shallowing.

'After waiting for about an hour at anchor, the mist gradually cleared to reveal that we were well out of the main channel and had in fact been attempting to sail up a beautiful sandy beach! With the help of the flooding tide, we soon reached the little harbour, dropping the anchor just outside while I rowed ashore to enquire as to the best position for *Patsy* to dry out against the wall. The quayside was deserted, so I went into the nearest bar and spoke to the barman who directed me to a lady sitting in the corner. She was most helpful, pointed out the best place to berth and asked us to come back to the bar later on in the evening to meet her husband.

'Having seen *Patsy* safely berthed, we returned to the bar where there was quite a party in progress. We met the lady's husband who was the local solicitor and himself a keen yachtsman. It seemed that not many yachts ventured up to Dungarvan and indeed we were the first English yacht to come in that season so we were the centre of some interest. We were bought large quantities of Guinness and were honoured to witness for the first time a splendid Irish custom. At closing-time the barman solemnly went round bolting the doors and fastening the shutters and then continued serving as before. It was very late when we finally staggered back to *Patsy* and turned in.

'The next day was a Saturday. We were woken by our new-found friends banging on the cabin side reminding us that the previous evening they had arranged to pick us up and drive us to their home for baths and lunch. In the afternnoon they took us, via one or two hostelries, to see the new marina near the entrance to the estuary. I think they would have entertained us for the whole weekend such was their generous hospitality, but we had arranged to meet Colin that evening and so, amidst more rounds of drinks, we made our farewells.

'Colin was to stay with us for a week and help us on the long passage back to England. The weather had by now much improved, so, at 0830 on the Sunday, we slipped from the town quay and drifted down Dungarvan harbour on the first of the ebb. Our destination was the little fishing harbour of Ballycotton, just 15 miles along the coast. It was a glorious day, with a light head wind and it seemed a crime to use the engine.

'Progress was desperately slow (we were obviously being overcome by the local indifference to the matter of time) and it was 0115 when we finally nosed into Ballycotton having made good 15 miles in 14 hours – I cannot imagine myself or anyone else for that matter exercising the same restraint on a passage say from Chichester to Cowes! To our astonishment there were still sounds of revelry coming from what appeared to be the village hall where we were able to refresh ourselves with more of the black stuff until the bar shut at about 0230.

'On Monday we slept late and then spent a glorious day exploring the local countryside. Tuesday was another splendid day but a flat calm so en route for Cork we took the opportunity of swinging the compass. About noon a little wind came up and we were able to sail, entering Cork harbour in the late afternoon where we found a convenient mooring off Crosshaven. In the evening, with some diffidence, we entered the hallowed and opulent premises of the Royal Munster Yacht Club. In spite of our scruffy attire, we were warmly welcomed and delighted to discover that the first drinks for visiting yachtsmen were on the house! Later on we had an excellent and very reasonably priced meal in the club dining room.

'With a tinge of sadness, the next day we bade farewell to the Emerald Isle. After dining again in style at the yacht club, we left Crosshaven in the last of the light bound for the Scillies. It was a still night, but dawn brought a gentle north-westerly wind allowing us to sail for most of the following day. The wind fell away again in the evening and once more we were on the engine, finally reaching the anchorage in St. Mary's at about 11.30 on the Friday morning. It had been an uneventful passage of 150 miles lasting some 37 hours.

'We had to wait on board *Patsy* for about 3 hours before a Customs Officer made an appearance. We spotted him rowing towards us in a fashion that suggested he had been having a very good lunch at one of the local pubs. He climbed on board with some difficulty, and then sat down in the cabin where

THE CUSTOMS OFFICER

he extricated the relevant forms from his briefcase. Before starting on the paperwork, he decided the call of nature could be put off no longer and staggered up on deck again. He planted himself on *Patsy*'s narrow side deck, where he stood unsteadily, oblivious that he was in full view of the whole town. At that moment a fishing boat went past at some speed and the effects of the wash pitched him head first into the water! We struggled to pull him back on board, doing our best to smother our laughter as he insisted on returning below, streaming water everywhere. Having completed the documentation, he departed without saying another word.

'The weekend was wet and windy so we stayed anchored in St. Mary's, but by Monday the wind had moderated a good bit although it was still dull and raining when we sailed for Newlyn on the Cornish coast, which we found with some difficulty in poor visibility. Colin left us there, and Martin and I sailed on to Helford and then to Falmouth where Martin also had to leave. With 3 days to wait around for my new crew, I spent the time happily doing a few minor repairs, cleaning and provisioning the boat.

'I was enjoying the luxury of a sleep-in, when I was woken by a shout of "*Patsy*, ahoy!". An old school friend was alongside in a small motor cruiser. Although it was some years since I had recounted to him past adventures in *Patsy*, my friend had remembered the name. He invited me to a party that night in St. Mawes. In those days we had as a tender an 8ft pram dinghy with a small sail, and as the weather was fine, I decided to make use of it to get to the party. This involved a daylight passage of about one and a half miles from one side of the Fal estuary to the other. This I accomplished without difficulty. The party was a good one, and it was about 2 a.m. when I emerged into a very dark night, having rejected various offers of overnight accommodation. I found the dinghy, hoisted the sail and set off back across the estuary. There was a perfect breeze. Ahead I could see the welcoming lights of Falmouth and I was feeling really rather pleased with myself until, with an awful bang, the dagger board struck an unlit rock just outside St. Mawes harbour. I pulled up the board, and floated free; then, considerably sobered, I sailed a lot further out to sea before heading over again for the Falmouth lights. I found *Patsy* without difficulty and turned in.

'Next morning, to my horror, I discovered that the dinghy was awash and only its meagre built-in buoyancy was keeping it afloat. I managed to bail it out sufficiently to row it ashore where I could examine the damage. The impact of the dagger board striking the rock had split the centreboard case, and only my weight at the aft end of the boat had kept the crack above the waterline. This had saved me from sinking in the estuary during the previous night's passage! As I carried out an effective temporary repair by fixing a G-clamp across the front of the centreboard case, it slowly dawned on me just how close to disaster I had been.

'My crew arrived that evening and we had some excellent downwind sailing during the following week, reaching Chichester as planned by the weekend.'

CHAPTER 9

# SHORT CUT TO BISCAY

I N Chapter Seven I have written that the west coast of Brittany is our
favourite holiday area. It can, however, take a long time to work the boat
along the north coast, through the Chenal du Four which is an area
notorious for bad visibility, and then on round the Pointe du Raz, past Pen-
marc'h and into the Bay of Biscay. At any stage of the journey there or back,
one may be delayed several days by the weather, as David was in 1963 when
he waited a whole week to round the Pointe du Raz on his way down to Biscay.
It was, therefore, with considerable interest that we read a magazine article,
published in 1964, about an inland waterway route linking the north coast of
Brittany with the west coast.

Although Brittany's canal system was built over a hundred years ago, the
southern exit into the Vilaine river was blocked after the last war by a bridge of
sunken boats. Since then, a fine new suspension bridge has been built just
upriver of La Roche-Bernard. The June issue of 1965 *Yachting Monthly* stated
that: 'Yachts drawing less than 4ft 1in can sail from the Channel to the Atlantic
without having to pass round Brittany. A waterway system directly connects
the North and South of Brittany, making it possible for small and medium-
sized yachts to reach the Atlantic without having to follow the inhospitable
coast of Finistère or to affront the violent currents and westerly winds of
the area.'

Since the route was opened up, we have used it on a number of occasions –a
marked contrast to our usual cruising with one eye on the barometer and the
other on the calendar! Armed with information from the magazine article
and notes from the Touring Club de France, I took over *Patsy* in St. Malo to
make our first attempt at Brittany's waterways. This was in 1965, when I was
joined by Noel (my brother-in-law) and his wife Betty.

Our first job was to remove the mast. The yacht club at St. Malo gave us the
use of a crane, and with the help of the one-armed boatman, we succeeded in
getting the mast down and securing it to two trestles – one of which sat on the
foredeck and the other on the afterdeck. Our solid wooden mast fitted snugly
into them at a height which gave us adequate headroom in the well. The
weather was lovely and the Basin Vauban was sheltered from the wind as we
prepared to enter the giant lock that leads into the tidal waters of the
Rance estuary.

Clear of the shelter of the Basin, the wind hit us broadside, kicking up short
steep waves and showering us with spray. We were totally unprepared for this,
and, as *Patsy* heeled over, we were in grave danger of losing the mast overboard. Noel had to hang on to it using all his strength while Betty retired

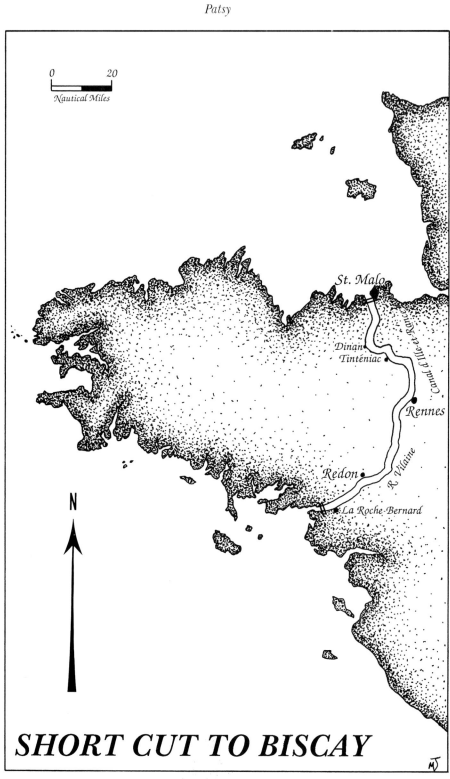

St. Malo

Dinan
Tinténiac

Rennes

Canal d'Ille-et-Rance

Redon

R. Vilaine

La Roche-Bernard

0    20
Nautical Miles

N

# *SHORT CUT TO BISCAY*

below feeling seasick. We only had a mile to cover, as far as the safety of the lock in the giant hydro-electric barrage that spans the Rance just above St. Malo and Dinard; but our progress was lamentably slow. I pointed *Patsy* upstream, but was unable to see much ahead because of the spray covering my spectacles. What a start to this peaceful (or so we had thought) alternative route to Biscay!

Once inside the barrage lock, they opened the road bridge and we passed into calmer waters beyond. We dropped anchor, and Betty came up from the cabin feeling much better. On the shore was a notice board which read RES-TAURANT, so in a rather shattered condition, we rowed towards it. In the restaurant they apologised that they could only give us cold salmon and salad followed by raspberries and cream with a bottle of local wine. They need not have apologised – I cannot remember a meal which I have enjoyed more!

The Rance river, between the barrage and the next upstream lock at Châtelier, is a great area for sailing in, not unlike the Norfolk Broads. There is, however, one great difference. Since the construction of the barrage (which was still in progress in 1965), the water level is maintained at fixed levels for several hours duration; but outside these hours the water level can drop 1.4m in 10 minutes as Électricité de France harness the power to drive the turbines!

There is a Usine Marémotrice pamphlet giving the time-table throughout the year for the maintenance of water levels in the Upper Rance. This information is also published daily in *Ouest-France* or can be obtained from a recorded message. I do not think we had this information in 1965 or a few years later when I was in the Rance with brother-in-law John. Without it one can be in serious trouble.

I remember that we had anchored for the night off St. Suliac, which is roughly half-way between the barrage and the lock at Châtelier. After supper we made our way ashore and called at the local café. There we had a very pleasant evening. John, who speaks no French at all, listened to the wartime experiences of the locals who had all been members of the Resistance; in return he told them of his adventures in the R.A.F. I sat at a table with an old man who told me over and over again how the last British visitor, after consuming a large number of drinks, had parted '*par le zig-zag*'. I think it was the only word of English he knew!

As darkness fell, we made our way back to *Patsy* and we all slept very soundly indeed. We awoke next morning to a lovely day. The sky was blue and there was not a breath of wind. I looked out of the porthole and the buildings of St. Suliac were nowhere to be seen! I scrambled into the cockpit and beheld an entirely different landscape from the day before. During the night, the level of the water must have risen by six feet or more; our anchor had dragged and we had drifted two or three miles upstream while we slept.

As recently as 1984, we got ourselves into difficulties through lack of information. Believing that the water level was rising, we had made our way up to the Châtelier lock which we found closed. Ken and I rowed up to the lockkeeper's cottage and asked him if he would open up. He replied in the negative, and went on to say that if we did not move off quickly we should be aground!

By the time we had got back, *Patsy* was already touching. Bill had tried hastily to fix the legs to prevent her rolling on to her side; but the situation was awful. Fortunately the level of the water rose again almost as quickly as it had gone down, and all was well; but if I ever go up the Rance again I will make sure I have on board the Électricité de France pamphlet which is headed *'Attention aux mouvements d'eau!'*

Dinan, inland of the Châtelier lock, is a splendid place in which to stay the night. The town is interesting and picturesque with good shops and all facilities. There is a small marina at the foot of a steep road which leads up to the town centre, or alternatively one can moor against the quay. In 1976 we were there on July 14th and enjoyed a magnificent display of fireworks from a ring-side seat. On the following day, returning down the Rance, Noel was at the helm. He had just recovered from a cataract operation, and his vision was still somewhat impaired.

'Is the course down the river clearly marked?' asked Noel.

'Yes,' I replied, 'but there are two French yachts just ahead of you – follow them.'

This he did, and about ten minutes later both French yachts went aground followed shortly afterwards by *Patsy*. She was on a mudbank, leaning towards the shore, and likely to remain there for at least four hours. It was the only occasion when I have been sailing with a bridge four, and valuable time was not to be wasted, so we laid out two anchors and rowed ashore in the dinghy, taking with us playing cards and scorers.

There was a steep path up the river bank, but we gained the top, passed through some fields and finally arrived at a main road which led up to a café-restaurant. The proprietor assured us that he could produce lunch; so we settled down at one of the tables for a bridge session. Our goings-on soon attracted an audience – a dozen or more of the locals who gathered round to watch the game, and were no doubt impressed by what they saw. (John and Noel are both very good players). After a splendid lunch, we made our way back to *Patsy* to find her afloat, lying to her anchors none the worse for her grounding.

Between Dinan and the 'summit' of the Ille-et-Rance canal, there are no less than 21 locks to be negotiated. When I first made this passage in 1965 with Noel and Betty, the procedure for passing through each of them was more or less standardised. On approaching, we gave a toot on our fog horn. At this a middle-aged lady would emerge from the lock-keeper's cottage, followed by children, dogs and sometimes chickens. She would then open up the first set of gates, and we would proceed slowly into the lock on the engine. There were then no ladders to enable yacht crews to scramble up to ground level, and we had to hoist Betty up to the top of the masonry and throw up our lines for her to secure.

The lady lock-keeper would then close the first gates and open up the sluices in the upper gates. The water would pour through in a torrent, and we would cry *'Doucement, s'il vous plaît!'* – but all to no avail. We found it very

IN THE ILLE-ET-RANCE CANAL

difficult to prevent poor *Patsy*'s topsides from bashing against the lock wall, and the end of the mast, protruding in front of the stemhead, was distinctly vulnerable. In recent years we have supplemented our fenders with some heavy-duty car tyres for the waterways.

At the summit are Les Onze Écluses or L'Escalier – a stairway of eleven locks all within a distance of a few hundred yards. Along this length, it was the habit of the lock-keeper to leave open the upper gates while she would mount her bicycle and ride on to the next lock which she had opened by the time we arrived.

In 1981, we made an unsuccessful attempt to reach the west coast. The maximum permitted draft is now 1.2m, so the actual waterlevel of the canals is critical as *Patsy* draws 4ft. The great droughts of 1976 and 1989 resulted in much of the canal system being closed because there was insufficient water. 1981, however, was a dreadful summer with more than average rainfall. This resulted in parts of the Ille-et-Rance canal silting up. Colin and his family reached Tinténiac (which is just below L'Escalier) where they became firmly wedged in a bank of mud which, on investigation, they discovered went from one side of the canal to the other, effectively blocking any further progress. They had considerable difficulty in extricating themselves, and then spent a couple of days cleaning up both the boat and themselves before returning to England.

I then went out to Tinténiac with Bill and Ken. We found *Patsy* in good order and in the company of another English yacht *Leander*, owned by Dr. and Mrs. Clements, who had also failed to get through. We contacted the waterway authority at Rennes who confirmed our worst fears – there was no hope of proceeding upstream for several weeks; so we had no option but to set off back home. Dr. Clements had also decided to return.

Because of all the heavy rain, there was a fierce downstream current which made steering difficult, but all went well until we rounded a sharp bend, beyond which a fallen tree blocked all but a very narrow passage. I tried to steer for this but *Patsy* refused to answer the helm and we crashed into the bank on the starboard side. I had hoped that the bank would consist of soft mud and bullrushes but, alas, we had driven into hard boulders and stuck fast. All our efforts to move her failed completely. We hoped that at any moment *Leander* might overtake and give us a hand, but there were no signs of her or anyone else. (Later Dr. Clements told us that they had been held up for two hours because the flood water was so high that the lock-keeper could not open the gates!)

Finally we got a line across the canal to a tree on the far bank. I shudder to think what would have happened if another boat had suddenly rounded the bend, but eventually we managed to get *Patsy* clear and were able to anchor. *Leander* passed and enquired if we needed help, but we said 'no', and the following day we both succeeded in getting back into the Basin Vauban at St. Malo. There, with the aid of the crane and help from Dr. Clements, we got *Patsy*'s mast up again. All, however, was not well – there were two very bruised patches on *Patsy*'s topsides and she was leaking.

During the next few days Bill was able to find in a dustbin a discarded piece of plastic sheeting, and with this we made a tingle which reduced the leaking to some extent; but it was not until we had worked *Patsy* along the north coast as far as Tréguier that we found a ship's carpenter who made a proper repair of the damage.

It would be a mistake to give the reader the impression that our recollections of cruising the waterways are for the most part restricted to groundings or other dramas. When we first passed through the canals, one could be underway for the whole day and never see another yacht. In the evening, after the locks had ceased operating, we would stop off at a small village or, if none was near, simply nudge *Patsy* into the bank and secure her lines round the trunks of a couple of trees.

The only blot on this idealistic landscape was Rennes, where the Ille-et-Rance canal meets the canalised Vilaine. This is the capital town of Brittany and, although there are some interesting old parts, the waterway passes through several miles of industrial suburbs. One motors through as quickly as possible to reach the attractive villages beyond. Then one reaches Redon, which is a small town with long quays where large seagoing vessels once moored and where the eighteenth-century shipowners' houses and warehouses still stand.

In 1986 David had sailed to St. Malo, returning later with his family to take *Patsy* on through the canals as far as Redon where they restepped the mast. In the yacht basin there Ken, Bill and I found her in a splendid berth. It was lovely weather and we set off in high spirits into the Vilaine river. From Redon to the sea is about 30 miles, with only one lock to negotiate which is part of the barrage that spans the river just below La Roche-Bernard. Once through the lock and in the tidal Vilaine, we became concerned that the engine was overheating until eventually it stopped altogether.

Ken managed to locate an engineer who spoke English and who dismantled the engine to find the cylinderhead gasket had blown; a new one would have to be located. All this was going to take some time, as the following day was July 14th and everyone was on holiday. After a lot of telephoning, a new gasket was despatched from Marseille; but this turned out to be the wrong size and eventually another had to be put on a plane from Copenhagen! Meanwhile *Patsy* lay at anchor in the middle of the Vilaine, off the village of Tréhiguier.

It was lovely weather. The anchorage was sheltered and the surroundings very pleasant. There was a good restaurant and a small shop – located in a converted garage, where Madame not only provided baguettes but also milk and butter and all kinds of vegetables. Ken and Bill thoroughly enjoyed themselves in spite of *Patsy*'s immobility; but I became frustrated. I suggested that while waiting for the spare parts to arrive, we might make our way down the river, into the estuary and out into the Bay of Biscay. But Ken and Bill thought to attempt this under sail alone would be foolhardy in the extreme.

I pointed out that it was not so long ago that characters like Claude Worth, Joshua Slocum and Hilaire Belloc had sailed in these waters in yachts not much bigger than *Patsy*, without engines and for that matter without echo sounders, direction finders, radio telephones or radar reflectors. But they were unimpressed with this argument. Eventually the parts arrived, and we were able to motor back to Redon which was a convenient place to hand over to Colin.

Returning to our very first waterway cruise in 1965 with Noel and Betty, the problem then was where to raise the mast. There was at that time no yacht basin or crane at Redon. There were no facilities at La Roche-Bernard where today there are two marinas and a crane. I was under the strong impression that we would have been able to step the mast there, having seen a photograph in *Adlard Coles Pilot* which showed a wharf and what looked like a crane. But when we arrived, the object in the photograph turned out to be a concrete lamp standard! When I enquired of a man digging in the front garden of his house, if there was a crane by the water, his emphatic answer was 'no'.

What was to be done? There was no point in going back up the river, so we pushed on downstream until we arrived at Tréhiguier. There, lying against a quay, was an open fishing boat, loaded up to the gunwales with mussels. The crew were standing knee-deep in their catch, unloading on to the quay. I enquired if they could possibly give us a hand in re-stepping the mast and they said they could do so if we came back when the tide was lower.

This we did, and about five fishermen rallied round to undertake the job. I endeavoured to point out what was needed to be done to refix the rigging but they pushed me to one side and confidently got on with the job which they completed most expertly. They would not take any payment but fortunately we had on board a dozen or more bottles of beer which they accepted gratefully.

# CHAPTER 10

# RACES AND RALLIES

*P*ATSY has entered for most of the Solent races organised by the Old Gaffers Association since they started in 1959, but alas her name has rarely appeared among the prize winners. I may be wrong, but my impression is that we have usually been unlucky with the weather. On the day of the race, there was often either the lightest of airs or half a gale of wind.

I remember one year there was a very light wind, but a strong west-going tide. In order to ensure that we were not swept over the line before the start, we anchored by the stern near the Committee Boat. Just after the five-minute gun had gone, a large ketch, completely out of control, swept down on the tide and carried us over the starting line! We watched the rest of the fleet get away on the gun, but not till some two hours later did the tide ease sufficiently for us to work our way back to the line and actually start the race.

Then there was the occasion when we got a good start and were up with the leaders as we passed the Medina river; here the jib halyard broke – and that was that. Another year there were yet again very light winds. Out of over fifty starters, only eighteen managed to get round the windward mark before the strengthening foul tide made it impossible. *Patsy* was the nineteenth; she and over thirty others had to retire.

I once watched the race from the windows of the Royal Corinthian Yacht Club at Cowes. It was a fine day with a fresh breeze and the fleet were strung out going westwards along the Hampshire coast. Suddenly, without any warning, there was a fierce squall with torrential rain. The view of the Solent was completely blotted out and remained so for over half an hour.

When it cleared, only one yacht was in sight – *Patsy*! The leaders had, I think, all been able to round the windward mark and then to cross the finishing line; the rest of the fleet had either taken shelter or had been dismasted or had used their engines to reach safety – all but *Patsy*, skippered on this occasion by my eldest son Peter, before he emigrated to Canada.

Richard writes: 'We could think of nothing else to do but to struggle on towards the finish and when the squall finally passed over and the visibility had cleared, we found ourselves approaching the finishing line; but no other competitor was in sight! As we crossed the line, a gun was fired and there were loud cheers from the committee boat although the rest of the finishers had passed two hours earlier! We were told afterwards that during the squall the wind was gusting to force 10.'

For that effort, *Patsy* was presented with the Laggards' Ladle of the Old Gaffers Association.

Another year, the race itself was uneventful but on the Saturday evening a

BRIGHTON MARINA, OLD GAFFERS RALLY, 1980

force 10 storm from the north hit Cowes harbour where most of the fleet were moored. There was some warning of the storm, and we took *Patsy* up river and moored off the Folly Inn. It was a wild night even in that sheltered part of the river. Of those boats that stayed at Cowes, almost all suffered serious damage and several were sunk!

My recollection is that many of the races particularly in the early years were spent making short tacks in the shallows, trying to cheat the strong Solent tides and struggling to reach the finishing line before the expiry of the time limit.

We did have some success at Brighton in 1980 when the owners of the Marina staged a Rally for Old Gaffers. There was a light easterly wind and a west-going tide. Most of the competitors sailed out to sea on a very long tack to the first mark; but Richard chose to make very short tacks almost up to the bathers in the shallow water near to the shore, and by doing so he won the race by a considerable margin. The prize was a barrel of rum!

Later that year, the celebrations of Drake 400 included a rally at Plymouth. The event included a passage race to Dartmouth. There was hardly any wind for most of the day, and the whole fleet were anchored for six hours or more somewhere west of Salcombe. *Patsy* finished at about 2 a.m., having had to beat into Dartmouth in the dark. Richard thinks that this must be the only event ever organised by the Old Gaffers Association in which there were allegations of cheating by some of the competitors who, it was suggested, had made use of their engines during the hours of darkness!

The Old Gaffers Association was started in Britain and then spread across

105

the Channel, but my impression is that the French do not usually take their Old Gaffers events so seriously as the English do. They are more concerned with hospitality. One year, *Patsy* entered for the Regatta at St. Malo, and turned out to be the only competitor from England.

Richard writes: 'The sailing was splendid and the organisers ensured that everyone, not least the visitors, had their fair share of prizes. The same year we sailed on to Perros-Guirec where another OG event was to be held. We arrived too late for the first race, but just in time for a very merry picnic lunch on the beach. By common consent, the start of the second race was postponed for an hour so that lunch could be properly enjoyed.

'The afternoon race was a resounding success for *Patsy*. Inspired by several glasses of wine at lunchtime, we tacked off on a "flyer" and found wind which eluded the rest of the fleet. We rounded the windward mark about half an hour ahead of the next boat and won the race comfortably. In the evening there was a great party and we were presented by the mayor with a magnificent book of Impressionist paintings and a dozen bottles of extremely potent local cider.

'The following day there was a passage race to Plymouth for those who wished to take part in the Drake 400 event earlier mentioned. Sadly only one other boat, a very large French yacht, had entered. Nevertheless we were formally started from just outside the Perros marina by the Mayor. It was a very hot day with hardly any wind and by evening we were still in sight of the French coast, although our competitor had long since disappeared over the horizon. The day was enlivened by one memorable incident. Our third crew member, who was not a regular *Patsy* sailor, reported that the loo was blocked. As it appeared (although never proved!) that he was responsible, he was ordered to unblock it. It seems that he had continued to pump even after it was obviously blocked, thus building up enormous pressure in the system. He was dressed in white shorts, white shirt, white shoes and even a white hat. He set to work with a spanner, and a few moments later there was the sound of a small explosion and he emerged into the well covered from head to foot in human waste. He has not sailed with us again.

'The race itself was really a non-event; but for some reason which now escapes me we refused to use the engine and finally made Plymouth about 40 hours after the start, having had to beat in through the narrow unlit eastern entrance to the Sound in the dark.

'No account of *Patsy*'s involvement with Old Gaffers' events would be complete without mention of the Rallies and Races in the Channel Islands in 1977 and 1978, sponsored by Bucktrouts, long-established suppliers of liquor to the local inhabitants. There were two excellent races: the first year a passage race from Jersey to Guernsey and the second a race around Sark. The hospitality was tremendous, and in addition every boat was given a case of booze which would have cost about £50 to buy in England. Despite this incentive, the second year was less well supported and sadly no further events were organised.'

The 1977 Bucktrout Rally had a great significance for Richard. En route to Jersey for the passage race to Guernsey, he anchored *Patsy* for the night in

Maseline Bay, Sark. There was one other yacht also anchored there, another Old Gaffer crewed by a young doctor with his wife and a friend of theirs, an architect student called Joanna. She and Richard met in the inn on Sark, again in Jersey and again after the race in Guernsey. They continued to meet after the holiday despite the fact that Jo was at College in Glasgow and Richard was living and working in Chichester. They were married in 1979 and have two sons, Edward aged 6 and William 4 who have already put in a lot of sea time on *Patsy*.

In 1987 we sailed over to Ploumanac'h to take part in the *Fête Maritime* there. There was a flat calm at the time the first race should have started. Quite a number of the Old Gaffers had no engine and could not get to the line on time, so the start was postponed. Whilst we were waiting, a French boat drifted alongside *Patsy*, and her skipper and crew, much to our amazement, leaped on board clutching a bottle of wine; this was duly consumed by all, and then they returned to their boat to await the start. When the gun finally went off, about a third of the fleet were over the line. I do not know how they decided who was the winner!

We enjoyed the fun of the regatta, and were happy to learn that we had actually won a prize (for the first boat to arrive at Ploumanac'h from abroad). At the prize giving, David decided that his son Toby should go up to the platform to receive it. When he did so, the president announced that *Patsy* was manned by three generations – Toby, David and me, and I was referred to as the '*doyen de la régate*'. My photograph appeared in the local paper next day!

For the 1988 Festival at Douarnenez, we arrived about mid-day and joined the fleet of about 800 Old Gaffers anchored or moored in the harbour. The town was so crowded with pedestrians that one could hardly make any progress along the quayside where we had arranged to meet Richard. He had arrived by car, having crossed the Channel by ferry; but how to find him among the thousands of visitors?

I fought my way through the crowds to a tent marked INFORMATIONS and did my best to explain my difficulty. From there I was taken to an office packed with telephones and typewriters where a most helpful official told me not to worry – he would put a call out on the loudspeaker. When he did this, Richard heard it and we were reunited a few minutes later!

Meals were provided for crews at long tables set up under cover in the fish market! The French certainly know how to serve good food, but I would not give them full marks for the organisation of the races. In the event, we missed both of them, but were told by other English competitors that they were somewhat chaotic. We did take part in a remarkable procession of almost 800 Old Gaffers on the final day. I then went home in the car with Richard, while Colin took over *Patsy* and sailed her back to England.

We had fully intended to take part in the 1989 Solent Old Gaffers Race and even set off to do so. Our reasons for not participating are described in the following chapter.

CHAPTER 11

# *PATSY'S* FINAL CRUISE

THE summer of 1989 had been a good one, and *Patsy* had made two trips across the Channel. Early in the season David and Richard took part in an Old Gaffers' Rally to Guernsey, and Richard and his family had a fortnight's holiday in glorious weather crossing to Le Havre, day-sailing westwards along the Normandy coast and making their way back to Chichester from St. Vaast.

On the 8th August, Ken, Bill and I embarked in Chichester harbour for a short cruise in the Solent. It was a fine day and we had good sailing until we had almost reached Cowes; then the wind freshened from the west, so we decided to start the engine.

We turned into Cowes where it was much more sheltered, and made our way up the Medina. David had recommended Island Harbour, a marina beyond the Folly Inn, and we decided to give it a trial. We turned in towards the entrance, aiming to put Ken ashore to make enquiries about berthing, but it was not easy to land on the jetty on the starboard side with the wind and tide against us.

Bill failed to edge *Patsy* near enough for Ken to jump ashore, so he decided to make a U-turn and have another go. He came hard round to port and promptly went aground! *Patsy* started to heel over. We attempted to get her onto the legs but failed to do so, and water started to flood in on the port side. Poor *Patsy* heeled over still further to port until the lee bunk was awash! Ken and Bill were able to get me ashore, where the harbour master generously offered us the loan of his motor cruiser which had three comfortable bunks.

On the next flood tide in the middle of the night, Ken and Bill attempted to refloat her, but so much water came in as the tide rose that *Patsy* remained firmly in the mud. The following day, the harbour master, with the aid of a huge pump, skilfully got *Patsy* upright and brought her into the marina. Still leaking badly, it was decided that she must be slipped. The Insurance Company's representative came and examined the hull. The immediate damage was not extensive but further investigation revealed that so much of the timber needed to be renewed that realistically the poor old boat was beyond repair.

After a great deal of discussion, we commissioned Hullmaster Ltd. to build a new hull at Island Harbour. When the work is completed, she will be an almost exact replica of *Patsy*, using the existing iron keel, the spars and much of the gear.

We intend to have a dinner to celebrate three things: (a) the launching of

*Patsy II*, (b) my ninetieth year and (c) the publication of this book. It has been fun to write and one hopes it may revive happy memories for those who have sailed with us. I hope, too, it may have been of some interest to those who, like Water Rat in *The Wind in the Willows*, enjoy messing about in boats.

THE LAGGARDS' LADLE

# APPENDIX

## TRACING HER ORIGINS

David wrote the following article which was published in December 1977 in *Small Boat* magazine:

We bought our 25ft cutter, *Patsy*, in 1955. She had been laid up for a couple of seasons at Itchenor Shipyard in Chichester Harbour, and was looking decidedly neglected with the black paint peeling off her topsides and her spars badly blemished by the elements for lack of varnish.

Nothing was known about this sturdy wooden boat when we took her over. She had no papers, only a name. Over the years, however, bit by bit, a little of her origins and past history have come to light. Although we cannot make any really positive claims as to her pedigree, delving into the past records of these traditional inshore sailing craft has proved a fascinating exercise.

The first positive lead came, quite by chance, not long after we had acquired *Patsy*. We had sailed into Cherbourg which, at that time, catered only in a modest way for yachts (mostly visiting English). We were invited aboard a large motor sailer whose owner, a Mr. Keane, remembered *Patsy* with some affection, for it was he who had bought her just after the last war and converted her from fishing boat to yacht.

*Patsy* had evidently been one of a fleet of fishing boats based at Rye, Sussex. She then had no name, just a number. As a fishing boat, she was open, apart from a foredeck, and had a large engine amidships. A Mr. Irwin Clarke (since deceased) had sold her to our Mr. Keane who had then spent a considerable sum converting her at a time when timber was scarce and very expensive. He built the cabin, lined almost the entire hull in oak, and replaced the large engine with an 8hp Stuart Turner.

With this newly acquired information, I paid a visit to the local Customs House at Rye, confident that the Register of Fishing Boats would have recorded a 25ft cutter belonging to Mr. Irwin Clarke, and perhaps give us another clue to follow up as to *Patsy*'s origins. I left empty handed, for Peter Irwin Clarke turned out to have been the managing director of the Rye Bay Trawler Co. Ltd., and his name appeared on almost every other page of the Register!

Our next clue came from marine artist, David Cobb, who had been commissioned to do some sketches of *Patsy*. I had ascribed her to Rye, but David Cobb wrote to me that her lines suggested *Patsy* was more probably West Country, and that she was possibly a refugee at Rye, for these inshore fishing craft tended to move around the coast a great deal.

For several years *Patsy* remained tagged 'believed to be of West Country origin', and then we had a real stroke of luck. We were pottering along the south coast, en route for Southern Ireland one day, and had the little drying Cornish harbour of Polperro abeam at around noon. The tide was just right for calling in for a couple of hours over lunch.

*Patsy* was squeezed alongside Polperro's old quay, and we were welcomed ashore by the harbour master, Jack Jolliff. He announced without a shadow of doubt that *Patsy* was an ex-Polperro Gaffer, probably the *Phyllis* or the *Lloyd George*. Had the main beam, just forrard of the original mast position, not been removed during the conversion, he reckoned he could have found a mark to establish who had built her and possibly even the date.

Jack Jolliff suggested we should call in at Fowey. There we could search through the Fowey (FY) fishing boat registrations which covered the area mostly used by the Polperro Gaffers between the west bank of the Seaton river and Dodman Point, including the harbours of Gorran Haven, Mevagissey, Looe (where the gaffers were built), Polperro and Fowey.

The next day had *Patsy* anchored not far off Fowey's Customs House, and me scanning the yellowing pages of the Register. The measurements of the *Lloyd George* were a fraction on the short side (24ft 5in) with a net tonnage at 4.95, and had to be eliminated as a possibility by the cancellation of the entry in 1938 when she was no longer being used for fishing.

The *Phyllis* looked much more promising. Exactly the right dimensions for *Patsy*, she had been built at Looe in 1912, and after two owners and the addition of an engine, she had transferred to Truro in 1939. The Registrar at Fowey followed up this lead with his colleague at Truro. Back came the reply: she had changed her name to *Sunbeam* with a closing entry in 1951 '*vessel sold outside of port*'. I had drawn another blank.

Some time later, I returned to Rye. The Registrar there, after my previous abortive search, had suggested I contact Jack Doust, the ex-harbour master of Rye. Jack Doust, like Jack Jolliff at Polperro, was an authority on local craft, with a remarkable memory spanning a good number of years. He very kindly worked through the local register and came up with a theory that *Patsy* was probably the former fishing boat *Boy Stan*.

A Commander Campbell-Shaw had brought *Boy Stan* to Rye in 1944 and she was last used for fishing in 1946. She was 25ft long, open except for a foredeck and narrow side decks, and fitted with a 30hp Kelvin Rickardo engine. The *Boy Stan* was converted to a yacht (cutter) and left Rye around 1947/48. Jack Doust believed that when she came to Rye she might have had an SS (St. Ives) registration.

Was *Patsy* originally the *Boy Stan*? The dimensions and deck layout described by Jack Doust certainly sounded right for a Polperro Gaffer. Jack Jolliff thought it a good possibility because he knew of several Polperro Gaffers that had fished out of St. Ives, and the boat name *Boy Stan* was typically Cornish. The records of the SS registrations would now have to be consulted.

I am still looking for the *Boy Stan*! Folio 105 of the St. Ives registrations, held at Newlyn, had no record of such a boat, although there were several other *Boy* registrations. It may be that she does appear in the register, but under a different name, for the names of boats and their owners changed frequently. This is a practical problem when attempting such a search, for these sort of alterations were not always recorded.

There is no doubt that *Patsy* is an ex-Polperro Gaffer. The National Maritime Museum produced drawings of a typical Polperro Gaffer which matched exactly *Patsy*'s lines and construction. She was probably built by Oliver or J. Pearce of Looe about 60 years ago, when carvel built gaffers were taking over from the local open, clinker-built, sprit-rigged fishing boats, many of which were wrecked in a great storm which practically destroyed Polperro's harbour in 1891.

### *PATSY*'S NEW KEEL

The following article by David appeared in August 1977 *Practical Boat Owner*:

My father had been sitting in the bar of the Cherbourg Yacht Club, awaiting his boat, since noon the previous day. Then the cable arrived – '*Patsy has developed serious leak. Have returned to Birdham.*'

Only once before, in 20 years, had our plans for extended summer cruising been thwarted. On that occasion it had been the weather; now things looked far more serious, for the future seaworthiness of our treasured gaff-rigged cutter was in doubt.

*Patsy*'s crew of three had set out from Chichester for Cherbourg in a fresh westerly breeze. Beyond the lee of the Isle of Wight, the old boat heeled hard over to port and water was soon coming in almost as fast as the bilge pumps could cope. It would have been rash to proceed further, so they limped back to Birdham Pool to find the cause of the trouble.

The hull of this 25ft, 6-ton gaffer is pitch pine planking on oak frames, but she is lined with oak boarding and filled with concrete almost to the level of the cabin floor, which made it very difficult to determine exactly where the hull was leaking. One possibility was that the upper seams had opened up as they are prone to, particularly after a hot spell.

We slung the loaded dinghy onto the end of the boom and laid *Patsy* over first to port and then to starboard. Although she made a fair amount of water, the test was inconclusive, but the concensus of opinion was that the keel bolts were no longer effective. That sounds simple enough, but those bolts were completely embedded in concrete and had not been examined since we first acquired *Patsy* over 20 years before.

There comes a point in the life of an old boat when the owner has to decide whether the cost and time spent in keeping her seaworthy is out of proportion to the value of the boat.

With serious leaking under any weight of sail, the only permanent solution to *Patsy*'s problem seemed to be to stiffen the entire hull, and replace the old keel with its suspect fastenings.

To have this work undertaken professionally would have been hopelessly uneconomical, and many owners faced with this situation would have sadly called it a day.

With *Patsy* it was different. Our 70-year-old cutter, once a working boat fishing out of Polperro, had great sentimental value. Perhaps more significant, we had sympathetic friends and relations in the iron and steel industries who agreed to lend a hand.

*Patsy* was duly hauled out of the water and laid up in Birdham Pool and, after removing the internal ballast, we set to work to break out the concrete below the cabin floor. What a job that proved to be! The concrete was as hard as granite, and full of lumps of old iron. Chipping away with hammer and cold chisel was hopelessly slow, so we hired a mechanical hammer which shook the hull from stem to stern and filled the eyes and throat with dust. Eventually we exposed the keel bolts, which proved to be almost non-existent, so badly had they corroded. Some years ago, on the recommendation of a surveyor, we had put iron straps round the keel which were bolted into the keelson, and these alone must have prevented the old cast-iron keel from dropping off altogether!

*Patsy*'s new keel was to be cast by the most modern manufacturing techniques, and one wonders what the West Country boatbuilder who built *Patsy* so many years ago, would have made of this automated, computerised process. One operation that had to be considered in the design stage was that of drilling the holes to take the keel bolts. The job of drilling down through the hog and the cast iron keel was made less formidable by casting rectangular holes transversely through the keel, well above the centre line, to take the nuts.

Another difference between the old and new keel were the proposed dimensions. We had always felt that *Patsy* heeled too much in a blow; even when just stepping on board, the movement was very noticeable. So this was our opportunity to achieve more stability by adding to the outside weight and reducing some of her internal ballast which consisted of 55 pieces of iron, each weighing 32lb, all wedged together on top of the concrete below the cabin floor. We calculated that with a keel four inches deeper at the centre we could probably halve the inside ballast.

But would the old hog be strong enough to support the additional weight of the new keel and transfer this to the frames? Clearly some sort of stiffening and distribution of the load was necessary. *Patsy*'s new backbone, connecting the keel and the floors was to be two lengths of 4 inch x 2 inch R.S.J., of channel section, heavily galvanised, and drilled to take the 3/4 inch diameter bolts which were to support the new keel. The original drawing included one complete length of channel-section R.S.J. for the whole boat, but fortunately it was realised in time that this could not have been slid into position without cutting the floor joists. In any case, two lengths were a much easier proposition, with the after, longer, piece passing through the floors horizontally, and the shorter piece angled to follow the upward curve of the keel and frames in the bows.

Our first plan was to have seven 5/8 inch dia. keel bolts, with the middle five passing through the old timber frames, strengthened with the steel floors. We then concluded the frames were too narrow (1 5/8 inch) to take a 5/8 inch bolt, and had to think again. We opted for 3/4 inch dia. bolts for extra strength, spaced between the frames but linked via the steel channelling. We also decided on nine 1/2 inch bolts to strengthen the hog, each passing through a frame and bolted down onto the steel channel. The keel bolts were ordinary mild steel bar with threads for nuts at both ends. The bolts in the hog were of galvanised mild steel inserted from the bottom, with the heads recessed in the hog so that nothing protruded to prevent a good fit of the keel. The 16 new bolts were to be staggered, port and starboard, down the hog to minimise rocking.

The five floors, manufactured from 1/4 inch steel plate and heavily galvanised, were tailor-made from hardboard templates, one for each wooden frame. Each had a flange resting on, and bolted to, its frame. This flange also carried the channelling which was bolted down onto the floor by one of the bolts from the hog.

A large central aperture in each floor for the channelling would also allow any water in the bilges to flow back to the pumps. We also made provision, by drilling a couple of extra holes, for electric cables etc. passing longitudinally below the cabin floor.

When all the new parts were ready for assembly, the hull was jacked up, the old keel was removed and the new keel bolts were inserted through the hog. The new keel was then placed in position and *Patsy* was lowered onto it. It was then simply a question of drilling down to the rectangular holes in the keel and bolting up.

There was considerable discussion as to whether or not we should replace the concrete in the hull. The timbers previously covered by the filling appeared to be perfectly sound, so we decided in favour, as the concrete would add to the stiffness of the hull and provide a better surface on which to rest the internal ballast. We gave all the timbers a heavy coating of Cuprinol, then hoisted up the concrete in buckets and laid it up to the level of the channelling, so that the keel bolts were still accessible.

The mechanical hammer used to break up the old concrete had naturally shaken up the whole hull and the drying winds had opened up the joints in the planking, so we re-caulked the seams using caulking cotton and a stopping compound of red lead, whiting and linseed oil. We then re-nailed all the planking from stem to stern and finally re-laid about half the original internal ballast.

*Patsy* was at last ready for putting back in the water. After 12 months on dry land, it was hardly surprising that on the first attempt to re-float her, she would take some water, but we were not prepared for the speed with which it poured in – almost as bad as before the operation!

After about a week in the water, still on the cradle, the intake was reduced, but still too great to risk putting to sea. It appeared that the new keel bolts were still leaking, so lead washers were inserted and these made some improvement. Even then, water was trickling in aft. We put some tingles on a suspect section of the garboard strake and finally poured hot pitch into the sump to a depth of about two inches. After that the leak stopped altogether.

The final test, which *Patsy* passed with flying colours, was under full sail. We chose a blustery day to shake her about in the stretch of water between Chichester Harbour entrance and Selsey. She made next to no water, and her performance was undoubtedly better with the deeper keel. The success of this sail was ample reward for the 12 months hard labour, and a few days later *Patsy* was at last cruising again – off to the north coast of Brittany.